## BREAKING THROUGH THE BARRIERS
## TO FAITH

It may be hard for ACAs to hear God's voice. Within their minds, the *shoulds* sound so strongly that they can override the voice of God. More important, they can be taken for the voice of God. First, since it was OK only to take care of others in the alcoholic home and not to value oneself, the ACA can make all choices—from vocation to marital partner—based on that *should*. . . .

When the ACAs break through the barrier to faith, they are capable of experiencing a close, warm, and meaningful relationship to God. They can use their pain to become compassionate, caring Christians to help other people who have experienced pain in their lives as well.

Bantam Books of Related Interest
See your bookseller for titles you may have missed

In Step with God: A Scriptural Guide for Twelve Step
    Programs by Paul Barton Doyle and John Ishee

A New Day: 365 Meditations for Personal and Spiritual
    Growth by Anonymous

Family Feelings: Daily Meditations for Healthy
    Relationships by Martha Vanceburg and Sylvia W.
    Silverman

A Time to Be Free: Daily Meditations for Enhancing Self-
    Esteem by Anonymous

Feeding the Soul: Daily Meditations for Recovering from
    Eating Disorders by Caroline Adams Miller

A Better Way to Live by Og Mandino

# HEALING
# FOR
# ADULT CHILDREN
# OF
# ALCOHOLICS

## Sara Hines Martin

BANTAM BOOKS
NEW YORK • TORONTO • LONDON • SYDNEY • AUCKLAND

HEALING FOR ADULT CHILDREN OF ALCOHOLICS

*A Bantam Nonfiction Book / published by arrangement with
Broadman Press*

PRINTING HISTORY
*Broadman Press edition published February 1988
Bantam edition / October 1989*

BANTAM NONFICTION *and the portrayal of a boxed "b" are trademarks of Bantam
Books, a division of Bantam Doubleday Dell Publishing Group, Inc.*

"ACA Work-Style Survey," Chapter 7, is based upon a survey by Sharon I. Eve
published in Focus on Family and Chemical Dependency, Nov.–Dec., 1985, pp. 24–25.
Used by permission of the author. Material in "Stages of Recovery," Chapter 12, is
condensed from Herbert Gravitz and Julie Bowden, "Recovery Continuum for Adult
Children of Alcoholics," Focus on Family and Chemical Dependency, May–June,
1985. Used by permission of the authors. Janet Geringer Woititz, Adult Children of
Alcoholics (Pompano Beach, Fla.: 1983). Used by permission. Co-Dependency rules
quiz, Chapter 4, is from Robert Subby, Co-Dependency and Family Rules (Pompano
Beach, Fla: 1984). Used by permission.

ISBN 0-553-28246-8

*Published simultaneously in the United States and Canada*

*Bantam Books are published by Bantam Books, a division of Bantam Double-
day Dell Publishing Group, Inc. Its trademark, consisting of the words
"Bantam Books" and the portrayal of a rooster, is Registered in U.S. Patent
and Trademark Office and in other countries. Marca Registrada. Bantam
Books, 1540 Broadway, New York, New York 10036.*

PRINTED IN THE UNITED STATES OF AMERICA

OPM   14  13  12  11  10  9  8  7  6  5

# Contents

# Contents

# Introduction

In writing about her Australian childhood, a woman recalls, "Once, when I was very young, a cyclone pounced from the north . . . and circled our jungle with its torrents of rain. It lifted the iron roof off the small room where I slept. I awoke, crying, to feel the rain on my face, and my father. . . ."

Let's stop the story there. What if the father in that home were alcoholic? Could he have helped the children in that crisis? He might have been drunk and asleep. He might have been awake, drunk, and raving; or, he might have been awake, but too sluggish and unaware to be of any help. He might have been out of the home for the evening, drinking. He might even have been home, sober, and acting effectively during the crisis.

What if the mother were alcoholic also? When a crisis, or a need on a lesser scale, arises in an alcoholic home usually the spouse and/or the children have to create their own solutions and save themselves without help from the father/husband, the one we expect to come to the aid of the family in time of distress. Can you imagine how devastating that type of situation is to the children?

Let's take that story in a different direction: What if the crisis of the moment were caused not by nature but by the alcoholic parent himself? What if the child waked to find herself under attack by her father? A Baptist minister tells of growing up with both parents alcoholics. He and his two younger sisters frequently waked to find their father slashing at them with a knife. Miraculously, the children escaped unharmed (physically, that is), but the mattress was riven in numerous places.

Cathleen Brooks, president of the National Association for Children of Alcoholics, says:

> Growing up with a chemically dependent parent can be like trying to survive a raging storm, alone, at sea in a very small boat. Children of alcoholics and addicts often live in frightened isolation, sure that no one understands, no one can help, and often equally sure that safety and peace will never come. As children, they usually develop strong survival skills—but have little sense of joy or freedom. As adults, they often cling to these rigid survival rules and may well pass them on to their children. Tragically, the majority of ACAs (Adult Children of Alcoholics) become alcoholics or addicts, marry an alcoholic or addict, or both. The storm rages on, generation after generation.

Approximately 28 million adults in the United States grew up in a home where at least one parent was alcoholic. First, public attention began to focus on the needs of alcoholics; later, awareness pointed to the needs of the spouses and the Al-Anon movement grew. Research shows that the children who grow up in these homes are affected, *for life*, by this background.

The term *Adult Children* comes about not because we are offspring of alcoholics but because we are children emotionally. When a person starts to abuse a chemical substance, his emotional and social development stops. When that person is a parent, the emotional and social development shut down for the entire family. When the children (adults in physical development) leave this home, they remain children emotionally until they get help to make breakthroughs in their personal growth.

In this book, we look at the areas in which growing up in an alcoholic home affects the adult, ways ACAs can become healthy adults in spite of this experience, and how they can deal with drinking parents.

Adult Children of Alcoholics don't need to go to a "pity party" or play a "blame game." The task for ACAs is to *identify* what happened—to see the connection between those experiences and present feelings and behaviors—and find guidance for healing. Many ACAs as well as other people say, "That's all in the past. Why dig it up?" The past has not died nor gone away. It lives, often in extremely subtle ways, in the life of the ACA. For example, *an alcoholic home affects the grandchildren as well* because they are being raised by parents who were raised by the alcoholic. If the ACA does not deal with the issues in his life caused by growing up in an alcoholic home, his children could find themselves caught in the negative effects, thereby perpetuating the hurtful dynamics of that original alcoholic home.

The story at the opening actually ended this way: "I awoke, crying, to feel the rain on my face, and my father's arms carrying me to safety." That father was a nondrinking man. In a healthy home, when the child finds herself in difficulty or danger, the parents use their awareness, strength, and skills to rescue the child. This behavior makes it possible for the child to grow up secure and emotionally healthy. In the alcoholic home, parental caring, protection, and intervention usually are missing. The adult child is badly in need of healing from the things done *to* him and the things not done *for* him.

Because the majority of alcoholics in this country are males, I use *he* for consistency when referring to the alcoholic without intending to imply that all alcoholic parents are the fathers.

The statements made about the alcoholic home and the Adult Children are what have been learned to be true, *generally*, through research and experience.

The material in the book is not a "one size fits all." As you read, identify what fits for you. The people (except for authors and other professionals) quoted in this book have been assigned fictitious names. A rather complete bibliography will help you in your search for other materials on the subject.

# HEALING
# FOR
# ADULT CHILDREN
# OF
# ALCOHOLICS

# 1

# The Way They Are

In this book, we do not deal with the moral issue of drinking, of whether or not a person ought to drink; we deal with the fact that people do drink. This book does not get into judging people who drink or are alcoholics. Neither is the book about alcoholics as such, but a brief understanding of who is an alcoholic is important as a base for understanding what childhood was like for ACAs.

There is no consensus definition of alcoholism. If the drinking behavior of a spouse, parent, or child adversely affects you, assume that he is an alcoholic and act accordingly.

Alcoholism keeps on developing whether or not the person continues to drink. He can go without drinking for years, but if he takes a drink, he may react as if he had been drinking all along. One man did not drink for twenty-two years, but after a few drinks he was having delirium tremens.

Here are some characteristics of the alcoholic personality, all of which have implications for the family members and for the home atmosphere.

—Sensitive, with little ability to handle emotional
   pain
—Angry

—Compulsive
—Paranoid
—Perfectionistic
—Controlling
—Rigid
—Self-centered
—Immature
—Jealous
—Dependent
—Critical and blaming
—Impulsive
—Fearful and anxious
—Depressed
—Moody
—Tyrannical
—Manipulative
—Irresponsible
—Impatient
—Self-deluding (filled with delusion and denial)
—Nurtures inferiority/grandiosity feelings
—Has poor communication skills
—Has difficulty handling emotional intimacy
—Has sexual problems

Harry, now in his forties, grew up in an Irish-Catholic family in New England in which both parents were alcoholic. He experienced substantial parental deprivation. He went to college primarily to get away from home. Neither parent wrote to him while he was away, and when he came home for his first Christmas vacation, the family had moved and had not informed him! The family occupying the apartment at the time knew where his parents lived. Harry tracked them down. "They were always moving—either they didn't pay the rent or the landlord complained about the collection of empty liquor bottles outside."

Harry has artistic ability, and some of his paintings hang on the walls of his parents' home. When he visits, his mother points to a painting and says with pride, "My Harry painted that picture. We gave him art lessons when he was ten years old." According to his memory, no art lessons ever took place. He begins to question his memories but sighs, "That's another example of my mother's delusion."

When Harry was a teenager, Paddy, a familiar drinking buddy of his parents, spent the evening. When Harry got up the next morning, Paddy was sitting on the sofa, very still. Harry thought that was strange, so he touched Paddy on the knee to wake him. He was dead! Harry roused his sleeping parents and his mother said, "We mustn't let the neighbors know!"

Harry chuckles, "The neighbors knew it all! But that's a good example of my mother's denial."

Dr. James Blevins, a recovering addict from prescription drugs, who works at Ridgeview Institute, Smyrna, Georgia, makes these observations about persons addicted to alcohol.

The public has an image of an alcoholic as a skid-row bum. This is far from reality. Ninety-five percent of all alcoholics are employed, many of them high in their businesses. A large percentage still have their families and may live in the best sections of town. The public myth hinders family members' identifying a parent or spouse as an alcoholic. If the heavy drinker is still functioning— employed, living with his family, and so forth—others often fail to recognize that the person's life is controlled by alcohol.

One out of ten persons who drink becomes alcoholic. Dr. Blevins points out, "We usually say, 'He is an alcoholic because he drinks too much,' when the reality is 'He drinks too much because he's an alcoholic.' Studies of the brain tissues of alcoholics show that these individuals are born with a predisposition to alcoholism. Something is going on in their brains that isn't going on in other brains. . . . Many children of alcoholics are potential alcoholics but never activate the addiction because they do not drink. If the person born with the predisposition drinks, he activates it."

A son of an alcoholic father proposed to a daughter of the same. He asked her to agree that they would never have children. "I do not want the responsibility of bringing into the world a child who has a hereditary predisposition toward alcoholism," he said.

A seventy-two year-old widow of a Baptist minister was having trouble sleeping following the death of her husband. Her physician son said, "Mother, some sleeping pills can be addictive so I don't want to prescribe any; why don't you drink a glass of wine just before bedtime each night?" She did and this woman who had never drunk in her life became an alcoholic within three months.

## Characteristics of Alcoholics

According to Dr. Blevins, if a person has two of the following seven characteristics, he is alcoholic.

### 1. Compulsive Loss of Control

The most severe alcoholic Blevins ever treated was a woman who drank only once a year, New Year's Eve. She would check herself into a hotel room and wouldn't stop drinking until she passed out. If she waked up, she drank again. One New Year's Day around six A.M. medics had to break down the door and take her to the hospital.

It is not how often the person drinks but the control factor when he does drink. Can he stop once he starts? For the alcoholic, the answer is *no*.

An alcoholic cannot control the timing, location, or amount of his drinking. Once begun, he will usually drink to the point of intoxication.

In addition to the loss of control over drinking, some

alcoholics experience a loss of control over their behaviors that is highly alarming to them. They become people they don't like; they behave in ways that are not characteristic of themselves.

What is the person's dependence upon alcohol? Can he take it or leave it? Does he build his life around the drinking? Audrey's father gets out the liquor at five o'clock each afternoon and declares, "Party time!" He has two martinis each day, and no matter the occasion he will not agree to do without it. Each Christmas is ruined for the family because of Dad's drinking. (Ruined holidays are standard in alcoholic homes.) Although this man does not drink heavily, he must have liquor on a regular basis.

Cheryl, a very successful career woman, dated an equally successful man a few times. When he phoned her, she noticed a slurring of his speech and the sound of ice tinkling in a glass in the background. He asked her if she would go out with him again. She gave him a list of positive strokes about his personality and his accomplishments but concluded, "You have a problem with alcohol. My father was alcoholic, and at one time I was in love with one. I will never get involved with one again."

"You're asking me to give up a lot!" he flared back, accusingly.

"I'm not asking you to give up anything. I'm simply answering your question about our future dating."

His dependence upon liquor was evident in the way he responded when someone said something that might *suggest* he give it up—Cheryl *demanded* nothing.

## 2. Withdrawal Symptoms when the Person Stops Drinking

## 3. Blackouts

A young woman, daughter of an alcoholic father, drank moderately in social situations. Soon she began to experience blackouts. Out of her background, she recognized the sign. Her father was in Alcoholics Anonymous, and she knew how helpful that organization is to recovering alcoholics. She entered the program immediately.

Alcoholics sometimes make promises or do things when in blackouts that they don't remember later. The family members are left to deal with the aftermath—physical wounds or broken promises—while the alcoholic denys that anything happened. A young child begins to doubt his own memory and his own perception of reality.

An alcoholic mother hit her seven-year-old son when she was drunk. The next day, when she asked him how he got that bruise and he said, "You hit me," she vehemently denied it. The boy doubted his own recollection.

## 4. Abnormal Tolerance—people who can drink others "under the table"

## 5. Physical Effects—damage to health

## 6. Psychological Effects—mild depression to full-blown psychosis

## 7. Social Effects

The social consequences are great. Gary Forrest says, "Problem drinkers invariably have people problems. The drinking activity produces severe problems in the important relationships in his or her life."

Normally a child develops socially by slowly incorporating or internalizing layers of society's rules and values. Chemical dependency, though, virtually halts or reverses this process by reducing alcoholics to an impulsive state where they interact meaningfully only with the chemical.

Alcoholics grab onto another person so they do not feel abandoned, but they do not relate to the other person. They treat others as objects. Janice's alcoholic husband retreats into his computer on weekends. She gets bored and talks about going out shopping or to visit a friend. He becomes highly anxious and demands that she stay. It helps him to just know that a warm body is there—under his control.

The alcoholic becomes the center of his own life. His ego is out of control, and he finds it nearly impossible to allow other people to enter deeply into his life. One of the reasons that Alcoholics Anonymous requires a person to acknowledge the existence of a Higher Power is to help the drinker begin to combat his egotism.

Growing up with an alcoholic personality does affect a child. The extent of these effects has only recently begun to be appreciated, and I want now to describe them.

# 2

# The Way We Are

## The Way We Are

Different factors determine how a child responds to the environment of an alcoholic's home. One survey suggests that children are affected most where both parents are alcoholics, less where the mother is the alcoholic, and least when the father is the alcoholic.

The child sometimes has a significant adult in his or her life who compensates for the destructive effects of the home. Sally's alcoholic father did not work regularly so Mother's family provided a home next door. When things got too hot at home, Sally went next door to nurturing grandparents and an aunt.

A child's position in the family can also make a difference. Julia, the oldest of six children of a mother addicted to prescription drugs (which leaves the same marks as if the parent were alcoholic) left the home before the mother's addiction progressed. Her younger siblings bear more scars than she. By contrast, Sheila, the youngest in her family, remembers spending lovely weekends swimming in the motel pool. She didn't know that her father's drinking had advanced to such an extent that each weekend, when he drank, the family left the home for safety. Sheila's oldest sister, who was fist-beaten by the father, has much different memories.

The child's individual personality makes a difference in the response to the situation. The more sensitive the child, the more severely he will be affected.

The way the alcoholic parent relates to each child can vary, also. The parent may focus most of his hostility on one child (or several children) and may relate in a loving way to one child (or several children).

Those who have studied alcoholic families say that *all children* are affected, no matter how the circumstances vary. An adult will say, "This doesn't apply to me because my mother divorced my alcoholic father when I was four," or "But my mother became alcoholic after I left the home," or "My alcoholic father died when I was a child." *It is the family system that is the root problem.* The family dynamics are at play, even if the drinking is remote.

## Messages Children Receive

These are some of the messages that children get in alcoholic homes.

You are alone. Nobody else is having the same experience you are.

It's your fault.

Your drinking parent is a bad person and could stop drinking if he wanted to.

Your drinking parent doesn't love you because if he (or she) did, he (or she) would stop drinking.

Things will never get any better. The drinking will never stop.

It's OK only to help my parent. I am not worthy of help and no help is available for me.

Dr. Claudia Black reports that schoolchildren of drinking parents have:

—poorer physical health than the norm
—more absences
—lower grades
—greater physical fatigue
—greater emotional fatigue

# Common Behavior

Forrest lists the most common traits of behavior that he has observed in the lives of those who live with problem drinkers. He presents them in the order he observes their surfacing in the course of the relationship. Although his book is written primarily for spouses of alcoholics, the information applies to the children, also.

## They Deny the Truth

Alcoholics engage in self-defeating behaviors, and anyone in a relationship with a drinker begins to do the same thing, usually beginning with denial.

## They Act Out the Problem

*Acting out* is a psychological term for the behaviors a person gets involved in when he tries to cope with internal emotional stress. These behaviors can be impulsive, immature, and irresponsible.

## They Become Reformers

They expend energy in trying to get the drinking to stop.

## They Become Isolated

Members of the family often withdraw from other people. Forrest states that the spouse of an alcoholic usually suffers more from loneliness than the alcoholic. The drinker sometimes has drinking friends.

**They Give Up**

Most people who live for years with a drinking person reach a level of chronic neurotic depression. They feel lethargic, uncomfortable, and have different physical complaints and chronic fatigue. Many women take refuge in overeating.

**They Go Crazy**

Most people living for a long time with the drinker begin to show severe psychological and physical ills, including madness.

Those who have studied ACAs have enumerated some personal qualities and behaviors that result from growing up in a home with a chemically dependent parent. The following list is not exhaustive, and not every ACA exhibits every quality. Pick those that apply to you. Most ACAs have trouble accepting or admitting their own accomplishments. Criticism, angry people, and authority figures scare us. We tend toward perfectionism, compulsive behavior, and dependence. Often, we assume responsibility for more than we can handle. When life is flowing smoothly, we live in fear of coming trouble; we come alive in crisis. Our sense of responsibility is acute, and we often assume responsibility for others. Indeed, we find it far easier to care for others than for ourselves. We are often very lonely, isolate ourselves from others, mistrust our own feelings and those of others, and do not easily express our feelings. At the same time, we fear emotional abandonment and will endure a hurtful relationship rather than be left alone. Sometimes we feel as if we have been victimized by people we know and society. All too often, we confuse pity with love and find ourselves strongly attracted to hurting, needy persons. We are haunted by the fear that our parents' drinking may have damaged us. Many of us become alcoholics, marry one, or marry a dependent personality. Finally, we usually have difficulty in standing up for our legitimate rights.

Janet Geringer Woititz, in *Adult Children of Alcoholics* (Health Communications, Inc., 1721 Blount Rd., Ste. #1, Pompano Beach, FL#33069, 1983) gives this list:

1. ACAs guess at what normal behavior is.

2. ACAs have difficulty following a project through from beginning to end.

3. ACAs lie when it would be just as easy to tell the truth.

4. ACAs judge themselves without mercy.

5. ACAs have difficulty having fun.

6. ACAs take themselves very seriously.

7. ACAs have difficulty with intimate relationships.

8. ACAs overreact to changes over which they have no control.

9. ACAs constantly seek approval and affirmation.

10. ACAs usually feel that they are different from other people.

11. ACAs are superresponsible or superirresponsible.

12. ACAs are extremely loyal even in the fact of evidence that the loyalty is undeserved.

13. ACAs are impulsive. They tend to lock themselves into a course of action without giving serious consideration to alternative behaviors or possible consequences. This impulsivity leads to confusion, self-loathing, and loss of control over their environment. In addition, they spend an excessive amount of energy cleaning up the mess.

ACAs become hypervigilant. Because of the lack of safety in the home, either physically or emotionally, they learn to "scout out the land," protecting themselves. They become adept at reading facial expressions and all types of body language and at discerning voice tones. In one family, everyone could tell by the shiny look of Dad's face that he was drinking! They then governed their actions accordingly!

As a result, ACAs become reactors, devising their course of action in response to the danger signals. They lack the ability to be self-directing because they learned to operate in reaction to whatever was happening at the moment. Whatever plan the child might have set up, he learned to throw it aside in favor of safety for himself or for another family member.

Dr. Claudia Black says that an ACA's reality may change every thirty seconds. The children learn to adjust rapid-fire and to feel no emotional response. Black illustrates with an experience out of her background. Her parents owned a tavern that was located next door to the home. On Saturday nights, the children amused themselves by watching the goings-on at the tavern out of the front window. When that got boring, they watched TV.

One night Claudia, her boyfriend, and her brother were watching TV when an abrupt knock came at the door. Claudia answered it, and a stranger asked, "Do you have any deodorant?" Claudia responded naturally, "Sure," and got the can. The man sprayed under his arms and left. The three resumed watching TV, with Claudia and her brother giving no reaction to this unusual episode. After a few minutes, her boyfriend, who did not come from an alcoholic home, asked, astonished, "Who was that man?"

Claudia answered, genuinely puzzled, "What man?"

The boyfriend answered, exasperated, "That man at the door."

Claudia gave him a withering look and said, "What's it to you?" and turned her eyes back to the screen. She and her brother were accustomed to handling inappropriate behavior without question and without even knowing it was inappropriate.

Black points out that ACAs *learn to tolerate the intolerable,* and they lose their ability to identify intolerable or inappropriate behavior as such. Even if they have an inkling that something isn't right, their feeling that they have rights is at such a low level that they brush aside any inner protests with, "Oh, well, I won't say (or do) anything about it."

It is not surprising to find ACAs who are highly intelligent, capable, and functioning well in life, yet who think they are insane. They get such incomprehensible, confusing messages from their parents (and this spreads to siblings) that these individuals conclude it is *they* who are the crazy ones. A thirty-three-year-old woman who held an administrative post in her work, the only female among male executives, joined one of my support groups. At the end of the first evening, she said, "I can't tell you how much the support here has helped me. I had concluded I was crazy because I couldn't find anybody else who feels the way I do. Tonight, as I talked, I saw heads nodding around the room and understanding looks in others' eyes. For the first time in my life, I can begin to believe that maybe I'm not crazy after all."

Karen, also thirty-three, an electronics engineer, makes the payments on her alcoholic mother's home. She also puts her husband through medical school. Karen's brother is wealthy, but he does not help their mother at all. The response Karen gets from Mother is that Brother is wonderful and Karen is terrible, the response Mother has given the children all their lives. Karen, too, came into a different support group saying, I think I'm crazy." As group members said to her, "I experience you to be sane and intelligent." Karen said, "Thank-you. You have given me a great gift."

Sadly individuals go through life thinking they are crazy when it is the family system they deal with that is crazy. ACAs often fail to realize their full potential because their energies are consumed by inner stresses. ACAs get into "overs." They overachieve, overeat, oversmoke, over-work, overexercise, overspend, are overconscientious, over-protective. They develop addictions of different types: to sex, pain, eating, religion, power, money, spending. Spending money can be used as a "fix" to handle painful feelings and can give the person a "high," similar to individuals who use drugs. Sometimes the addictions are positive: running, learning, reading, and so forth.

A friend of mine received a phone call from a thirty-three-year-old woman who belongs to a religious group that forbids watching TV. Her father learned that she had bought a TV, so he ordered her to sell it. The call to my friend was to ask, "Do you know of anyone who would buy my TV and let me keep it here and watch it?" The woman wanted to be able to tell her father that she had obeyed him, that she had sold the TV!

"She's addicted to TV," my friend commented. "All she does is watch it."

While completing my studies toward the MS degree in counseling, I did a practicum in a halfway house for recovering addicts and alcoholics. One female resident spent her waking hours, except for mealtimes, in front of the TV. She was unable to organize her life enough to get a job or participate in activities with other people. She was a TV addict.

## Tendency Toward Alcoholism

A woman called me asking for the statistical probability of children of alcoholics becoming alcoholic. "My husband was alcoholic," she explained, "and my four grown children insist on drinking. I want some facts to give them so they will stop."

"All of them are at high risk," I told her. "But it will probably be useless for you to give them statistical information. If you were to tell them that 50 percent of them would become alcoholics, each child would feel sure that two of the others were vulnerable, not himself. That seems to be the way people operate, in general. They think the other person will have cancer, get hit by a car."

These are the facts I was able to give her, though.

—ACAs are four times as likely to become alcoholic as the normal population.

—Members of the medical profession are thirty times more likely to become addictive than the normal population.

## The Roles We Play

Sharon Wegscheider describes the five roles that members of the alcoholic family take in order to adjust to the chaotic environment that exists. They take these roles to preserve the family system at all costs. In nature, there is a law of homeostasis—the push to maintain equilibrium in a system. The family system operates under this law—when something is out of balance, family members adjust to bring about balance and to keep the family intact even at their own expense.

The purpose of the role taking is to protect and take the focus off the main problem-person. In the alcoholic home, that is the drinker, called the *Dependent*. If he had to face the consequences of his unhealthy, irresponsible, and antisocial behavior he would be overwhelmed. He rarely has to face those consequences because the people around him step in to protect him. That process is called *enabling*.

Wegscheider observed over ten years of working with alcoholic families that all five roles are played and that everyone plays a role. No one escapes. If there is a small family, members double up roles. In a large family, more than one person may play certain roles. The choice of roles is a subconscious one. Roles can take place in all troubled families—any time a family is under stress. But in alcoholic families the roles are more rigidly fixed. They are also played with greater intensity, compulsion, and delusion.

Anyone playing a role is not being honest with either himself or others.

Role changing can take place. A person may get tired of playing a role and may start behaving differently, which throws him into a different role. Circumstances can change the role for the person. Wegscheider, the oldest child, was the family's *Hero*. When she left home, her family did not understand and they viewed her as the *Scapegoat*. In her new family, she finds herself tempted to play the *Enabler* for her three children. But in the alcoholic family, individuals usually get trapped into their roles, and they are forced by unconscious pressures to conform to those roles. They become the roles they play. The position in the family determines the role more than the personality of the individual. An only child takes on parts of all the roles—he may play them all at once or he may take turns. The longer a person plays a role, the more rigidly fixed in it he becomes.

The one closest to the alcoholic, the spouse, becomes the chief *Enabler*. The Dependents lean on their spouses who act out of love, loyalty, shame, and fear. If the Dependent is unmarried, a roommate, parent, or friend can take the role of Enabler. When the Dependent is a child, a parent often serves as the Enabler.

Enabling behavior begins gradually, without the awareness of the Enabler. She (or he) feels she has no alternative but to take over in light of what is happening. She excuses and defends the Dependent's behavior and eventually becomes locked into denial, just like the Dependent. She may call his boss and report that he has the flu when he actually is drunk or hungover. She will cover for him to relatives and friends. She takes over responsibilities when he becomes less participatory in family life, pleads with him to quit drinking, threatens to leave, destroys the liquor, and so forth. But all of her superresponsible behavior only enables him to go on drinking.

She is standing between the Dependent and the crises that would follow from his drinking. Without realizing it, she is protecting him and making it easy for him to continue.

Other people may see the Enabler as nagging, sarcastic, and unpleasant. Anger is her primary feeling. She feels tired, physically and emotionally, and powerless to change things. Denial prevents her seeing the realities of the total family situation, and she begins to suffer from delusion.

If the Enabler has a belief in God, she may retreat into her faith, may even become a religious fanatic. She may sit and wait for a miracle rather than take an honest look at things and develop a strategy for change.

The way out is for the Enabler to admit her helplessness over the drinking. One of the best ways she can do this is to join Al Anon, an organization for family members of an alcoholic. She must risk confronting the Dependent and get help for the entire family. If he refuses her help, then she must pull out and help herself and the children.

The *Hero*, usually the oldest child, grows up closest to the Enabler, so he behaves the way she does. He learns that the way he can help most in the family is to be very, very good. He may be an A student at school, become president of the student body, be an overachiever in general.

The Enabler, leaned on by the Dependent, leans on the Hero. We would expect that a person who is being leaned on by two people from above would crumple, but the Hero manages to keep his feet firmly planted on the ground and carries the load. The *Mascot*, usually the youngest child, tugs at the Hero for attention. The Hero is thus leaned on from one direction and pulled at from below, but he manages to stand. His primary feelings are inadequacy and guilt.

The Hero usually leaves the home at a younger age

than the others because of his overachieving characteristics. Maybe he graduates from high school at an early age because of his scholastic ability. His striving will continue throughout life, and his primary feelings of inadequacy and guilt will stay with him unless he gets help. He feels some anger, too, because he must work so hard to be good. And because he is "good," he will bury the angry feelings, which makes him feel more guilty.

Because the Hero is hypercritical, it is difficult for him to form friendships. And if he should let his guard down with others, his own suppressed feelings might reveal themselves.

Wegscheider says, "Even though the Hero's intellect may be highly developed, his mind—that higher faculty where our wisdom is lodged—is severely crippled. His behavior is governed, not by truth and good judgment, but by false perceptions and an overriding compulsion to pursue a goal (of perfectionism) that is out of reach."

Spiritually the Hero may appear to be a saint. But a person with truly mature spirituality acts out of his own value system. The Hero is good because he feels he must be to please other people and/or God.

The Hero's pain does not usually show to the public. In marriage, he sometimes becomes an Enabler, helping to perpetuate a sick family system.

Sometimes the Hero gets weary from overachieving and, as an adult, begins to behave in a way that is atypical of him and baffling to those close to him. He may abandon all his good behavior and go in the opposite direction. Mack took care of his younger brothers and sisters while the parents drank. At fifty, he started drinking heavily. After being a model husband and father, he signed up for active military duty and didn't even tell his wife! He was acting like a rebellious adolescent running away from home. Elaine, an outstanding attorney, checked herself into a psychiatric ward for depression at thirty-seven. She said, "I'm just tired of always pushing myself." She refused to work any more.

The *Scapegoat* role is usually taken by the second child who cannot compete with the perfect first child. The Scapegoat finds himself being attracted to other frustrated children, who are so greatly in need of attention from their parents that they will do anything to get it. Negative strokes are better than none at all.

To outsiders it seems as if the Scapegoat doesn't care—since he brings humiliation on the family—but he is the most sensitive child in the family. His primary feeling is hurt. He is acting out the stress felt in the entire family. By his behavior, he is trying to call the family to take action about the wrong that is going on in the home.

Another of his tasks is to keep the parents' marriage intact. As long as he keeps them united, going to the principal's office or court, to take care of him, they won't focus on their conflicts. Some examples of Scapegoats would be teenagers who get into dropping out of school, drink, drugs, pregnancy, or running away from home. Although it is hard for parents to see this at the time of the misbehavior, this child has the potential for being the one who is closest to them after the conflicts are resolved.

Because his behavior calls attention to him, the Scapegoat is the child who usually gets the most help. He is the one who visits the counselor's office at school, gets bailed out of financial disasters by his parents, is the focus of family discussions, and so forth. His chronic low self-worth and self-destructive tendencies may lead him to commit suicide. The Enabler and Hero may come across to him as goody-goodies, so he may sympathize with the Dependent.

Males and females may assume the Scapegoat role. School teachers and others in the community have a difficult time understanding the outlandish behavior of the Scapegoat because they have usually dealt with the Hero. "What in the world is wrong with that boy?" they ask.

"His older brother is the most outstanding student in school and that boy is in the principal's office every day." Someone may add, in a lowered voice, "I know his father drinks too much, but his mother is the sweetest woman in our church."

The *Lost Child* (or Forgotten Child) is usually the third child. He handles the chaos in the family by withdrawing and his primary feeling is loneliness. Staying in his room, he reads and avoids conflict as much as possible. He does not feel close to either parent. The Lost Child also feels worthlessness but little anger, in contrast to the Scapegoat. His personality is essentially passive. On the positive side, his solitude can provide a setting for developing a rich personal spirituality.

In school he does not distinguish himself in any way. The Hero calls attention to himself by high academic activity and the Scapegoat does the same thing by getting low grades, but teachers often do not notice Lost Children. If a teacher is asked if Joe Burnette was in the fifth grade class several years ago, he or she will not remember him. Because they are withdrawn, Lost Children may be labeled as slow learners or socially retarded.

A Lost Child can become a Lost Adult, never finding his niche in life. He may have difficulty finding and keeping jobs. He has few friends and rarely finds a suitable marital partner. Sometimes he disappears literally. In my work, many of my clients say, "That's right! Uncle _____ just disappeared. No one knows what happened to him." The Lost Adult may drop out of sight and reappear several years later. The family had assumed he was dead. The Lost Child may get lost in drug use, although he may binge rather than become dependent, as the Scapegoat.

Wegscheider says, "The Hero and the Scapegoat are both propelled, in opposite directions, by an irresistible compulsion, while the Lost Child makes his entire existence one grand denial. Now it remains only for someone to express fully the family's delusion. That someone is the *Mascot*, usually the youngest child."

The parents and older children overprotect the Mascot who senses that much is wrong in the family and becomes highly anxious. No one confirms his fears, so he begins to wonder about his own sanity. He learns to develop his wit and charm and becomes the family clown. His task is to help the family relax when the tension gets too great. He is jumpy and nervous and can be labeled hyperactive, which can lead to his being put on Ritalin. This means that he, like the alcoholic parent, is dependent upon a drug.

The Mascot's primary emotion is fear. He may even fear for his life. One grandchild of an alcoholic often thought she had a fatal illness. A headache meant that she had a brain tumor, a minor virus meant she was going to die.

The Mascot is a manipulator and is lonely even while being the center of attention through his antics. People do not take the Mascot seriously, which hurts. Even though he may be intelligent, he usually does poorly in school. It is hard for him to develop any spirituality because he cannot sit still long enough to read or look within himself or commune with God. Until the Mascot has counseling, he can never learn to cope with stress. As stress builds up, he may escape into delusions or phobias. The Mascot is the family member most likely to develop serious psychiatric problems. He may also handle stress by becoming chemically dependent or attempting suicide.

In dysfunctional families, members place heavy emphasis on roles rather than personhood, and relate to one another out of that stance. "A father should . . ." "A woman's place . . ." "This is woman's work, (man's work), . . ." and similar expressions echo through the halls of these homes.

Relationships can change rapidly as roles change. The

old saying, "No matter how well a woman knows a man before she marries him, she wakes up the next morning and finds herself married to a total stranger" can be true in an ACA's marriage. Nothing was too good for Marsha while Frank pursued her for marriage. But on the honeymoon he delivered his lists of oughts for a wife. Many of the rules dealt with important issues in a marriage, yet he had never brought those up during courtship. Whether consciously or unconsciously, he waited until she had the title of wife before mentioning them. And he did not discuss the list—he issued orders. Marsha was not free to be herself and develop her role as Frank's wife as an expression of her personality—Frank's family decreed that Marsha behave a certain way, according to their expectations and rigid rules. Marsha, an ACA, felt she had no option but to submit. She would protest from time to time about the way Frank and his parents treated her, but he would respond in an intimidating manner and she, on cue, was intimidated and hushed.

Marsha complained that Frank did not help raise their four daughters, and he defended himself by saying, "If we had sons, I would get involved with them." He further said that he did nothing that the girls would be interested in helping him do. When Marsha suggested that they help him wash the car, he stated dogmatically, "That's man's work." He had worked out a neat system for avoiding any parental responsibility based on his definitions of male/female roles. He and his wife worked together in their business, where she put in equal hours. But when they came home, the housework, cooking, and child care were hers, according to Frank's code. The father/husband sat in a rocking chair and read the newspaper.

Rhonda was in graduate school and Lane's mother became greatly upset when she learned that her son was typing his wife's term papers. If Rhonda had done the same for Lane, that would have been fine!

Extremes of behavior are the norm in dysfunctional families. In a functional family, the husband and wife are fairly well united in their values and the ways they operate. The children, then, stay more to the middle because they do not feel the need to take roles to keep the family in equilibrium nor do they feel the need to rebel. In the dysfunctional family, we find one daughter who has "never been kissed" and another who is promiscuous. We find a police officer and a son in trouble with the law. We find a child who becomes super successful in his career and one who can't hold onto a job. We find one who leaves home to establish an autonomous life and another child who can never break away from the family. One child may secure a graduate degree, another might drop out of school and not even get a high school diploma.

Take a few moments and sketch your family of origin. What role did you play? What roles were played by other family members? Did the roles ever change? If so, note the changes.

After you finish that exercise, try making a sketch of your present family. What is your present role? What roles do your current family members play?

If you are like most ACAs, these exercises will reveal that you and your current family have been affected dramatically by the circumstances of your childhood. This is not your fault; you were reared in a dysfunctional home, a subject to which we now turn.

# 3

# The Root of the Matter

When I first learned of the study of Adult Children of Alcoholics, I heard, "The Alcoholic home is thus-and-thus . . ." and "We children are thus-and-thus. . . ." For me, that information was not enough. I like to know *why* things are the way they are.

The basic problem is called *dysfunctional family living*. Here are several possible examples: a home where a parent is chronically ill; a home where a parent or grandparent is mentally ill; a home where a parent is emotionally ill, including chronically depressed; a home where one parent dies and the surviving parent is so overcome by grief he or she is unable to cope with the parenting tasks; a home where physical and/or sexual abuse takes place; a home where suicide has taken place; a home where a child was adopted; and the rigidly religious home. (This last category surprises many people because nothing is specifically *done*, as in the other categories. This type of home produces similar dynamics because children are not valued for themselves but are raised by rigid rules. The father, if a minister, may neglect his family while carrying out his work. The children can get the feeling they must make the parents look good in the eyes of the community.)

In summary, these families focus on a problem, addiction, trauma, or some "secret," rather than on the child. The home is shame- and blame-based.

In a normal home, the main tasks of the parents are: their work, their relationship to one another, and raising the children. In the dysfunctional home, the task of childrearing is given short shrift.

The alcoholic and/or chemically dependent home is considered to be the most extreme example of dysfunctional family living. The statistics for sexual and physical abuse double in homes where a parent is alcoholic. Statistics for suicides are extremely high in alcoholic homes as compared with nonalcoholic ones. Eighty percent of teenage suicides take place in these families. Many phobics come from these families. (Many phobics are not diagnosed accurately because they drink to medicate their phobia-related stresses and thus become labeled as alcoholic.) Most anorexics and bulimics (primarily females) are children or grandchildren of alcoholics. Mentally ill individuals come primarily from these homes. Whatever category of sickness exists, it is made worse (or even caused by) alcoholism.

Of course, dysfunctionality can occur in a normal family for a period of time during a crisis. For example, if a parent dies, the other parent might go through a period of being unable to adequately parent, then might return to a highly adequate level of parenting. A forty-year-old woman told me, "I know nothing about my father who died of cancer when I was eight. When we children would come in from school each afternoon, Mother would be lying on the couch looking sad. So we would say, 'Let's don't talk about Daddy because it makes Mother cry.'" That daughter, the oldest of four children, became so dysfunctional that she stayed home from school two months that year. She developed an abnormal fear that her mother would die too. After a period of time, the mother emerged from her grief-stricken state and resumed her previously healthy style of parenting.

Other dysfunctional parents do a great deal of damage to children through faulty parenting; if those parents were also alcoholic, the abuse may well intensify. All of us have impulses from time to time that, because we are sober, we are able to hold in check. When a person drinks, he or she loses impulse control, which paves the way for that person to act on those destructive, perhaps brutal, impulses. Being a parent is difficult enough when we are at our best, which would include being sober. If a parent is addicted to a substance that changes his or her personality and behavior, the results could be disastrous.

All of these homes deal with similar dynamics. The basic issues for the children are *abandonment* and *rejection*. Cathleen Brooks says that emotional abandonment is the worst kind, even more devastating than physical abandonment. Emotional deprivation is the rule in these homes. The parents are not able to take care of parenting tasks because they are overwhelmed by their own problems. Therefore, nobody raises the children. The children do not get an opportunity to be children.

When I make these statements in a workshop, some ACAs find this information hard to believe. It doesn't seem to square with what happened in their homes with regard to the behavior of the sober parents. The ACAs also hear these statements as criticism of the sober parent. Often that parent prepared meals on time, may even have been a "super parent," perhaps one of the best members of the church, and admired in the community. No criticism of this parent is intended. The sober parent often behaves impeccably in the presence of the alcoholism. But, knowing what we do about what the spouse is coping with, it is impossible for her or him to give adequate attention or depth to the parenting tasks. The sober one often tries to make up for the absentee or abusive spouse, trying to be both mother and father. When this happens, the children do not get adequate mothering or fathering.

In family life, four terms are especially important—*boundaries, roles, coalitions, and enmeshment*. When these are violated, dysfunctionality occurs. In speaking of dysfunctionality, think of a continuum: a family may be slightly to severely dysfunctional, and, as mentioned earlier, may become temporarily dysfunctional.

A male who has healthy ego boundaries, a strong identity, and a solid sense of self is able to attract a woman with similar personality strength. They are then able to effect a strong marital bond. That erects a firm boundary line around their marriage. The boundary serves the purpose of privacy and freedom for the couple to conduct their marriage and their family life according to their values. The boundary line keeps them in and it keeps certain people out.

Who might try to invade the boundary line and enter the marital space? In-laws might try to come in—to tell the couple how to live their lives, to drain emotional nurture from the couple that belongs to the marriage, or to try to pressure their child to continue to put them first. Children might attempt to come between Mom and Dad. An outside party might feel attracted to one partner and attempt to draw that person outside of the marital space.

Where might the partners go outside the marital space? To a parent, to an affair, to work, into the children's space by sexual and/or physical abuse.

In a functional family, everyone is able to operate within his or her expected role. This does not mean that the husband and wife fulfill traditional roles insofar as the husband earns the living and the wife stays at home and keeps the children. It refers to the fact that the husband/father feels comfortable in these roles and is able to carry out duties expected by our society—contributing to the welfare of the family through earning a living and protecting and providing for the children. This husband feels so secure in his personal identity that he could be the househusband while the wife earned the living—*if* that is what the two of them agreed upon. The wife/mother likewise understands that her role is to be a companion to her husband and a nurturer and provider for the children, and she is capable of fulfilling these demands. She also feels secure enough within herself to work outside of the home if the two of them agreed to that.

Sometimes the question arises from women: Should a mother put her husband or the children first? If the husband and wife put each other first and create a strong marital bond, the children will get what they need.

Single mothers also ask, Can I have a functional family if there is a divorce? If the divorce is clean emotionally, the family could be more functional than while the couple was married. If, however, the man and woman continue to fight each other—and especially, through the children—dysfunctionality takes place. A recent survey showed that the majority of divorced spouses continue to fight each other through the children for as long as five years after the separation.

Just as the adults in a functional home understand their roles, the children also understand theirs—they are the ones in the family to be taken care of. The boundary line around them is strong, and they do not need to fear that a parent will cross it to abuse them. In this home, everyone knows who he is, feels comfortable being that, and stays in the expected role. The children do not get a message to leave their role and go up into the parental role to take care of the adults.

A male with a fragile ego, unclear sense of self, emotional immaturity, and low ability to relate intimately (share his feelings with another person and get close to another) attracts a woman who functions on a similar level. They, therefore, are seldom able to bring about a strong marital bond from the beginning. That leads to a fragile boundary line being erected around their marriage. In-laws may come in, marital partners may go out, emotionally if not literally.

The children in these homes often have weak personal identities. The boundary line around the children is fragile. Parents can invade the children's space for inappropriate emotional nurture and for sexual and/or physical abuse.

Cathleen Brooks states that the *alcoholic is the neediest person emotionally in the family*. He, the Dependent, leaves his role as father/husband and becomes the emotional infant of the family. He may be functioning on a high level in the eyes of society; he may earn a high income. (Both of Cathleen Brooks' parents were alcoholics and her father was the richest man in their county, holding a position high in corporate life.) Where both parents are alcoholics, they line up side by side in claiming the space of the emotional infants of the family.

*The spouse*, when nonalcoholic, is called the Co-Dependent. The alcoholic is dependent upon the bottle and the spouse is dependent upon the alcoholic. She, devastated by living with alcoholism and coping with unmet needs, *is the second neediest person in the family*.

The children come last.

When the parents abandon their roles, that forces the children up into the parental role, bringing about role reversal which causes great insecurity in the children. Firm boundaries give children security, and when boundary lines are moved or violated, great insecurity results. Emotional chaos takes place. When I first heard of the chaos in the alcoholic home, I thought of frying pans flying through the air. Some children of two alcoholic parents report that literally happening. In many alcoholic homes, though, no violence takes place. Instead, the parents abandon their roles in a very subtle sense. On the surface, everything may look in order: The alcoholic parent may be earning an excellent living, the family may be living in a beautiful home, and meals may be prepared on time. But the children get messages, in subtle ways, that they must be and must behave in certain ways in order to keep the parent(s) comfortable. This is severely damaging to a child's sense of well-being.

When the role reversal is overt, children literally raise themselves and sometimes raise their parents. Children put a drunk parent to bed and mop up vomit. The child may comfort a drunken parent who cries, saying, "I'm no good, I'm bad." Children may raise younger brothers and sisters, buy groceries, prepare meals—activities that belong to adults. This has nothing to do with children having chores in the home—the issue is that children often have responsibility for functions that only adults should have. The children undergo considerable anxiety when they are unable to carry out these duties on an adult level. Many such children are reprimanded for not performing—and for not performing perfectly—tasks for which they have no capabilities.

Cathleen Brooks, from age nine, came home from school in the afternoons, prepared dinner, and supervised the younger children. To add to the stress, Mother's response to Cathleen's activities was mixed. Mother was always "napping" when the girl came home each afternoon. If Mother's nap left her rested, she would teeter down the stairs, lay a hand to her brow and sigh, "Oh, Cathleen, I have so much to do."

Cathleen would reply, "Mommy, you make a martini and sit down and rest." That was before Cathleen knew the connection between martinis and Mother's behavior. All she knew was that whenever Mother was under stress she would make a martini to help her relax. Cathleen later learned to pour out her parents' liquor and to make up concoctions that resembled liquor to pour back into the bottles.

On other days, though, Mother would wake cranky and yell at her daughter, "Who the ___ do you think you are? *I* am the woman of this house. *I* will cook dinner. You're grounded for a month! I know what goes on when you go to your friends' houses." The baffled daughter would go to her room, tremendously confused about how she had offended. There she would make charts on self-improvement, all items dealing with matters over which she had little or no control. "Be happy." "Do something about the space between your teeth." "Brush your teeth more often." "Smile more."

Because of the emotional chaos caused by role reversal, control becomes a big issue for the children. The child is often placed in control. The child may be told, "Watch your daddy and don't let him drink while I go shopping." Or, a child may be sent with Daddy to a bar with the instruction, "Don't let him drink too much." One man said his mother always sent him with his father with no overt instructions but with the hope that the child's presence would influence the father's drinking. In response to such assignments, the child attempts to control his environment and can't. So he attempts to control himself, starting with his emotions.

The neediest one experts the greatest amount of control in the family. Sometimes this is done overtly, with noise, perhaps with violence or fanfare. It can be done in a very subtle manner also, through manipulation and the use of guilt. An outsider might never guess the powerful control that the quiet parent has over the other family members. The controlling person is not in touch with his own power and actually feels that he is a victim of the other members.

In a dysfunctional family, the members are not in touch with their personal power in general. If lined up in a circle and asked "Who has the power in this family?" each would point the finger to the person next to him. The parents feel controlled by their children, the children feel controlled by their parents, the spouses feel controlled by each other. The wife and children may tremble around the father, yet he might feel quite powerless as an individual, which is one reason he behaves in such an intimidating manner. He may complain all the while that no one in the family does as he says when he actually has almost total control. Power struggles, rather than relating, take place in these families all the time. One-upmanship becomes a practiced art, and each member fears becoming the underdog because he does not trust the top dog. Family members become very defensive. Winning, rather than relating, becomes the goal.

In the alcoholic family, much intimidation and misuse of power occurs. The strong use their strength to overpower the weak rather than help them. The children grow up to be both easily intimidated and intimidating.

*Coalitions* take place in a dysfunctional home. That refers to who buddies up with whom, who feels comfortable with whom, and who feels the need to align himself with another family member in order to be safe from another. Coalitions occur when the boundary lines move. In a functional family, any family member is able to feel comfortable when alone or when alone with any other. In a dysfunctional family, certain family members feel anxious when alone or when paired with certain others.

For example, an alcoholic father and the oldest daughter are buddies. If the mother ever criticizes the father, the daughter bristles and defends her father. The girl has actually been placed in the position of "wife" by the husband. In some instances where this happens, sexual abuse may take place, but often the union is based upon an emotional devotion. The husband is giving to this daughter the devotion due his wife—he has placed the daughter in the number one position in his life.

Only the husband has the power to place his wife in the "wife" position. She cannot put herself there. Until the husband stations his wife in her rightful spot, the wife remains a child in terms of the family's structure, and the children cannot go through adolescence emotionally. No one in this family grows up.

The mother and three younger children huddle together for support. In this family, there is no physical abuse, but the grouping takes place for emotional comfort. When I dealt with this woman as a counselee, I saw a well-groomed, attractive, successful career woman, but I had the feeling I was talking with a twelve-year-old child. She simply had never grown up.

In the alcoholic home, the one who abuses a substance stops maturing emotionally, and this dynamic spreads to the entire family.

Sometimes the boundary line remains drawn around the husband and his mother. He has not *individuated* (achieved his own identity separate from hers). He remains a child and wants his wife to be a mother figure. A wife can also remain attached to her father.

A thirty-seven-year-old woman, daughter of two alcoholic parents, drew boundary lines in every direction in her family of origin. She said, "I knew when to buddy up to this one and when to buddy up to that one, etc." She could never relax and feel secure in any one position—she had to keep a sharp lookout to know when to shift position for emotional safety.

*Enmeshment* refers to the extent to which family members are involved with each other. *Overenmeshment*, which is unhealthy, happens when members are overly involved with one another. They are watched, their every move observed and commented upon, usually critically. Sometimes individuals feel pressure to move as a unit and have no life independent from others. In a healthy family, differentness and independence of movement are allowed and respected. In an unhealthy one, family members can feel a lack of freedom to develop friends and pursuits apart from the family.

For example, in a nonalcoholic home, a mother felt very hostile toward her epileptic fifteen-year-old daughter, Sheila. The woman felt ashamed about the girl's condition, had many fears about Sheila's development, and behaved negatively toward her child most of the time. One day the girl lingered in the bathroom for five minutes. When she emerged, the mother accosted her. "What were you doing in the bathroom so long? I know you didn't need to go because you just went a little while ago!" She acted as if the girl had done something to be guilty of. Probably the girl was doing the very normal fifteen year-old thing of looking at herself in the mirror—maybe combing her hair a different way, experimenting with makeup, wondering "Am I pretty?" The mother watched the girl so completely that she even kept track of how often the girl went to the bathroom! A child that is overwatched becomes self-conscious.

Another example from a nonalcoholic home involved a mother who was partially deaf and was considered "strange" in her rural community. (Deaf persons can become paranoid because they cannot hear what is being said and can think they are being talked about when they are not. People also tend to stop talking to deaf persons because communication gets to be frustrating, which increases the deaf person's feelings of isolation. Keeping family members within the field of vision can become important to the well-being of the deaf person because then she knows what is going on.) In this family, whenever teenage Tom went to the outhouse, the mother became anxious and called out, "Where's Tom? Where's Tom?"

Another family member would say patiently, "Mother, he has gone to the outhouse."

In these two examples, members of the families couldn't even take care of biological functions without the mother trying to keep them under her control. We could label those families as overly enmeshed.

A woman told me about her sister's family. The husband and wife had a business and the five children worked there. "They are so close," my friend said, "all except the sixteen year-old son who committed suicide." It could be theorized that he needed to do that in order to get out of the smothering family! Along the way, the sister learned that her husband was having an affair. All that family "closeness" was a delusion.

At the opposite extreme is a family where *under-enmeshment*, or *disengagement*, takes places. In this system, the family members rarely gather as a group, and especially, they do not gather for enjoyment and sharing. When both parents are alcoholic, underenmeshment is common—perhaps no dinners are prepared and no parents appear at the table sober. A child may not show up for dinner and no one notices, cares, or comments upon it. These members may have little interaction with each other.

In an unhealthy family system, people believe "What I do makes another feel what he feels" (which is impossible). "I make Daddy unhappy and then he drinks." In these families, members do not take responsibility for their own feelings and behaviors. They say to each other, "You make me mad," rather than "I am feeling angry at you." Also, members feel overresponsible for the others and underresponsible for themselves.

In a healthy family, the members come together in a balanced way—*by choice and for enjoyment and for mutual help*. In an overenmeshed system, emphasis is on *we should* be together. In a home where the mother was hypochondriac and the father clinically depressed, the only son felt free to marry only because he brought his wife to live in his hometown where he could still carry out the obligations his parents, especially his mother, placed on him. Often he said to his bride, "We must go to visit Mother because she will get her feelings hurt if we don't." When the couple visited the parental home, the atmosphere was funereal. No one seemed to enjoy being together. No one laughed or relaxed. The mother's anxieties did diminish when her son was there because she believed "A son's place is with his mother." The son's anxieties diminished because Mother withheld her attacks about his neglect as long as he was literally in her presence.

The young couple visited there frequently but always under the injunction of "We must." They felt no choice and they experienced no enjoyment. Eventually the wife asked her husband why he continued the routine since it seemed as if he dreaded the visits and felt no pleasure while being there. He answered, "Because I feel guilty when I don't." And the mother reinforced those feelings of guilt. Whenever the son did not give her the attention she wanted, she screamed at him, "You don't love me!" To protect himself from attacks and from the resulting guilt feelings, he continued going home.

Three types of family systems exist with reference to how free the members interact with outsiders. In *the closed system,* no one comes in from the outside and those inside don't go out. The alcoholic family usually becomes a closed system for several reasons. The family members feel embarrassed when they invite friends over so they stop doing it; the alcoholic usually cuts off contact with other people, and the spouse accommodates him or her and stops going to functions as well. It might be actually unsafe for family members to bring in friends. ACAs get a message (usually subtle) that they must not leave, that they must stay and take care of the others in the family.

An ACA explicitly told her husband to stay home with her because her anxieties shot so high when she was alone. Each began dying as persons and the marriage itself began to die because no life was coming in from the outside.

*The troubled system* is one in which there is some flow between the inside and outside, but there are significant difficulties with family members feeling free to bring outsiders in and feeling free to leave. Sometimes there is enough health from the sober parent's side of the family that the children have interaction with outsiders modeled before them.

In *the open system,* a healthy system, there is much coming and going. Family members go out to visit friends and relatives, to pursue activities independent and maybe different from anyone else in the family. Outsiders come in. A strong network develops between family members and others outside the nuclear family. This family is not paranoid about others. In a strongly closed family, a church member came to visit and later the hypochrondriac mother snapped to her family, "Mrs. ____ came snooping around today." A friendly visit was given twisted, suspicious motives. In an open system, family members trust outsiders and welcome them into their lives.

Dysfunctional alcoholic families are cut off from the outside by the desocialization of the alcoholic. Dr. Douglas Talbot, director of Ridgeview, a treatment facility, says that gradually the alcoholic shuts out the world: church and community contacts first; then friends; hobbies, sports, and leisure activities; peers; then distant family. Finally, he shuts out his nuclear family. Dr. Talbot concludes with a statement that is very important to ACAs: *"Deficiencies in these six areas are believed to exist in all members of the chemically-dependent family."*

I am aware that this information sounds like all gloom-and-doom and that I need to answer the question, "Now we know what dysfunctional family living is—tell us how to go about it the right way." So here it is.

Essentially, if you will turn all the negatives listed previously onto the flip side, you will have the positive ways families operate. Here is a list of some characteristics of a functional family.

It has a positive climate. The atmosphere is nonjudgmental.

Each person is accepted with regard for his/her individual characteristics.

Each person operates within his proper role.

Members care for each other and affirm each other.

Family members use open and direct communication.

The family produces children who can separate; individuation (becoming an individual apart from the parent) occurs.

Families come together out of choice.

Members operate within clear, firm boundaries.

The atmosphere is safe so that members can function spontaneously with humor and wit.

Intimacy is achieved. This requires people to make themselves vulnerable by their commitment and self-disclosure. They share personal secrets and fears while trusting the other persons to continue to care about their feelings. They also commit themselves to being careful of the other in the same way.

# 4

# Co-Dependency and the Dysfunctional Family

## Co-Dependency

The alcoholic home is one example of a *co-dependent* system, defined in these ways.

It is a dysfunctional pattern of living and problem solving which is nurtured by a set of rules within a family system. The rules are unwritten and unspoken but are very powerful.

It fosters exaggerated dependencies and interferes with our process of identifying our feelings.

It is learned behavior that interferes with our forming relationships.

It is a psychiatric syndrome which results from ineffective attempts to cope with the addictive behavior of a chemically dependent loved one.

It is a pattern of learned behaviors, feelings, and beliefs that make life painful.

In this system, members develop co-dependent relationships rather than interdependent ones: they become entangled with each other and lean excessively on one another (or one leans too much and the other tolerates that imbalance) rather than standing as separate individuals and reaching out to relate to and help one another. No one in this system feels able to be an autonomous individual who conducts his life according to his own values and needs—he feels tied to the family and controlled by their values and needs. Co-Dependents connect with other emotionally needy individuals. When one Co-Dependent tries to escape, the other one panics.

Sharon Wegscheider defines Co-Dependents as all persons who (1) are in a love or marriage relationship with an alcoholic; (2) have one or more alcoholic parents or grandparents, or (3) grew up in an emotionally repressive family.

Anne Wilson Schaef says Co-Dependents have low self-esteem; are passive and do not take care of themselves physically, emotionally, spiritually, and/or psychologically. They compromise themselves, ignoring their personal morality. They are perfectionistic. They are dependent, out of touch with their feelings, self-centered, and focus on others rather than themselves.

The last two characteristics sound contradictory but make sense when explained. *Self-centered* refers to the immature quality of a child who has a limited view of life because of his lack of experience and input. He thinks he can control other people and events. If something happens outside of himself, he thinks he did it. The child often takes upon himself the blame for the parent's drinking. ACAs internalize events—if a crisis happens "out there," they think they did it. When a child develops normally, he gradually learns that he is not the center of the universe and that his power is limited.

*Focusing on others* means reacting rather than acting. It means feeling OK only to take care of others and feeling guilty about placing one's own needs first. It involves people-pleasing behaviors, making decisions based on the fear of what other people will think rather than making decisions based on one's own morality and desires.

In the alcoholic home, the Co-Dependent (the sober spouse) takes on the behaviors of the chemically dependent person without using the substance. The main expressions of co-dependent behavior are: repressed feelings; compulsive behavior; delusion and denial.

The children take their cues from the co-dependent parent and become, therefore, Co-Dependents themselves. The chemically dependent person is unable to handle feelings so he medicates his painful emotions. The Co-Dependent represses hers, and the children handle their feelings in the same way.

A Co-Dependent learns to do only those things which will get him the approval and acceptance of others. He gradually denies much of who he really is. At birth, the private self and the public self are equal in power. A baby, for example, is not concerned with what people think of him. If he has a dirty diaper that is odoriferous, he doesn't care at all how that comes across to other people. He does what he needs to do to take care of himself. (This does not mean to imply that people do not need to exercise control of their offensive behavior as responsible adults.) Yet, in the Co-Dependent system, by adulthood, the power of the private (real) self has shrunk and the public self has most of the power. One of our tasks as ACAs is to discover and release that real self within us that is the unique self God created.

Co-Dependents have not formed their own values— they have a contract with the community that says, "If you will tell me what is approved, that is what I will deliver." They go around with an earphone out to the outside world to get marching orders on how they are to behave, what they are to believe, what they are to feel, and so forth. They rarely know what they want or what they feel. Someone may insult a Co-Dependent and he or she can espond by feeling numb emotionally—whatever hurt he eels is quickly repressed or not felt at all.

Co-Dependents do not know how to make choices. In his type of home, the members do not learn that they have options. Submission to the authority figures (and to he system) is presented as the only way to respond. This leads to children being extremely loyal, even when such loyalty is not deserved.

Claudia Black, in *It Will Never Happen to Me*, says, "Members of the alcoholic family system act and react in manners which make life easier and less painful for them." Individuals in a Co-Dependent system can become very skillful at coping within the system and never give any thought to getting out.

To reduce and avoid tension in the home, families may act in ways which actually support or *enable* the alcoholic's behavior.

A woman and her alcoholic husband developed a business with her brother. He and his sister would cover for the husband at work. If he had an appointment and didn't show up for it, one of the co-workers would handle it. The alcoholic never had to experience the consequences of his actions. After twenty-five years of marriage, the woman decided to try to stop getting her husband to change and to work on her own co-dependent behavior. She joined Al-Anon and learned about *enabling* (unintentionally helping the Dependent to stay that way). She began to act differently and stopped protecting her husband. Before long, he entered a treatment program, and he has maintained sobriety for several years now.

A co-dependent system can exist in different situations: a business, a church, an entire culture. Such a system is the normal condition in a dysfunctional family.

# Rules in Dysfunctional Families

No couple ever sat down and decided, "These are the rules our family will live by. Number 1: we will not be free to talk about our feelings; number 2: we will not communicate directly." Yet, families all over the world live by similar rules, rules that have been observed and identified by those who have studied families. Adults from dysfunctional families marry others from similar families, sometimes of the same stripe but sometimes with a different label. For example, Hal's mother died when he was a child. Daddy lacked any significant nurturing skills and the family struggled along on every level, from preparing meals to emotional relationships. Hal suffered severe parental deprivation. He married Betsy, whose father had been mentally ill. Hal entered the ministry, and he and his wife created a rigid religious home.

When adults from dysfunctional families create new families, they almost always perpetuate the rules from their homes of origin. They do not know anything different; they repeat what was modeled before them and the way the parents interacted with them. Even when two individuals are highly motivated to establish a healthier style of family living and perhaps read books and take courses, the power of the earlier dysfunctionality is very insidious; the individuals often find themselves carrying on the patterns of relating and behaving that took place in their homes.

Stewart, child of an alcoholic father, married Eva, who recognized after their marriage that her father had also been alcoholic. Stewart, a ministerial student, is highly motivated to give his baby a positive home life. To the young daddy's surprise, as he (trying to be a good father), played on the floor with his eight month-old son, Stewart found himself feeling angry and jealous toward his baby. "He has what I wanted and didn't get. While I love my son very much and don't want him to have the negative background I had, those feelings come over me spontaneously." ACAs can make intellectual decisions about how they want to operate their lives and relate to others but their emotions and the patterns from the past can be powerful in overriding the intellectual desires.

Here are specific rules in dysfunctional homes.

## 1. It's Not OK to Talk About Problems

In the alcoholic home, this rule comes out as, "Don't talk." The "don't talk" rule can apply both inside the home and outside. This leads to extreme secrecy and lying. One reason for secrecy is that historically society has viewed the alcoholic as immoral, weak-willed, mean, or just crazy. These images have led to shame and embarrassment for the family and the alcoholic, so everyone tries to hide the "family secret." Sometimes a family denies that a parent is alcoholic within the home. Sometimes the family acknowledges this fact openly to each other, but the secrecy rule applies outside the home. Children catch on while still very young to observe the rule of silence.

Part of the child's need to deny is that she or he feels that the drinking is his fault. Madeleine, now in her fifties, recalls feeling, at age eight, "If I were a good child, then I would have a good daddy." She had received messages that Daddy, who drank, was bad, and she took on herself full responsibility for what he was. These children believe that if they're good enough, if they do enough, they can change what is happening. When they can't, they try to hide their failure from the world, and they feel guilty about their failure.

This rule causes ACAs to avoid their own problems and deny that they have them. *Denial*—pretending that what exists doesn't exist—is one of the strongest dynamics in the alcoholic home. At first, Madeleine disagreed that her family engaged in denial. "We didn't know the word *alcoholic* then, but we all recognized that Daddy's drinking was a severe problem and we all viewed him as a villain in the family." When asked if that openness applied to the community as well, she said firmly, "No. That was a different matter. Mother would have died before discussing this situation with anyone. (And everyone knew, of course.) There was no Al-Anon or any source of help in our rural community, but I feel certain that Mother would not have gone if there had been one. She would not have identified herself to outsiders as the wife of an alcoholic."

Madeleine recalls an embarrassing incident that took place when she was in the third grade and had a part in a small play at a PTA meeting. Her farm family did not own a car, so neither parent planned to attend. Daddy never attended those functions, even when sober. After the play was over, Madeleine took a seat beside a classmate in the auditorium near the girls' rest room. Soon Madeleine heard a familiar, very loud voice from the entrance door, to her back. It was Daddy, who usually drank only on weekends, and he was very drunk. He sat down and talked constantly to the person beside him, drowning out the meeting.

Madeleine's instinctive reaction was to start whispering rapidly, nonstop, to her friend, trying to cover up the fact that Daddy was there and behaving as he was. She had learned—by age eight—to deny, to keep the secret. It never occurred to her to say to the friend, "That's my daddy and he's drunk and I feel so embarrassed." Today, Madeleine says, "You know, that girl had no idea that was my daddy. The best thing I could have done would have been to keep quiet and she would never have known—and she probably didn't catch on to what all my chatter was about."

A current friend asked her, "Why didn't you go into the rest room for the rest of the evening and hide?"

Madeleine answered, "That never occurred to me. If it had, it would have shown that I had learned something about taking care of myself and my feelings. All I knew was to stay fixed and create a diversionary action to keep others from seeing what was going on."

Wendy Frederickson, alcoholism counselor and child of two alcoholic parents, grew up in Chicago in an apartment without air-conditioning. In summer, the windows always stayed open. If any ruckus started due to drinking, Mother would say, "Be quiet! We don't want the neighbors to know what's going on!" Of course, Wendy comments, everyone had a ringside seat on what was going on.

Denial in alcoholic homes can extend to areas other than the alcoholism. An alcoholic physician refused to acknowledge that his three children had hearing problems and did not get medical treatment for them. All have faulty hearing as adults.

Denial of marital problems is common in these families. The children can see that the parents do not have close relations, but the parents do not discuss their problems between themselves, and the children catch on to turn the other way when the parents quarrel or when the coolness between them is apparent. (This does not mean to imply that parents need to discuss their marital problems with, or in front of, the children. It can be very healthy, however, for a couple to inform the children that the parents are seeing a counselor to work on problems within the marriage.) Two married daughters from an alcoholic home were visiting each other. One said, "You know that Mother and Dad were very unhappily married."

The sister responded quickly in a rebuking tone, "I don't think you ought to say that." She had learned the lesson well: don't talk about problems. The sister who made the comment did not make a judgment about the parents; she simply stated something that was obvious to all in the family. The other sister heard the statement as a criticism of the parents and rushed to squelch further discussion.

*Avoidance* is another of the most prevalent behaviors

in the alcoholic home. The husband and wife lack skills to talk with each other about problems and feel uncomfortable doing so, so the child sees this modeled before him. He observes that his parents become uncomfortable if he breaks this rule by asking questions or making comments. Persons in these families will go to any lengths to avoid discussion of a problem or open confrontation. These family members rarely talk to each other about anything of substance; they chat about vacations, new clothes, progress in their careers, children's activities, but rarely about their feelings, especially their pain.

The individuals in these homes are judged rather than accepted. If they have something wrong with them or if they have problems, they are judged rather than understood or sympathized with. They develop strong masks rather than acknowledge their weaknesses to others and make themselves vulnerable to attack. Not only is it common for these individuals to withhold information from others about problems, they also deny to themselves that they have problems.

## 2. Feelings Should Not Be Expressed Openly

In the alcoholic home, this rule comes out as, "Don't feel." *Control* is a strong issue in the alcoholic home. Since feelings can't be controlled, the rule works to suppress them. Terrible things may be happening in the family, but members are expected to look and act happy, to push down negative feelings. The expression of feelings is extremely threatening. In this home, feelings are not respected and are betrayed.

Fredrickson tells about a particular incident in her home. Her drunk father pushed her drunk mother onto the coffee table. She lay on the floor bleeding. Wendy, the oldest child, instructed the two younger ones to call an ambulance. When it arrived, the father yelled at Wendy,

"Why did you send for this? Don't you think I can take care of my own wife?" He sent the ambulance away.

The next morning, both parents were sober. At the breakfast table, the main topic of conversation was what kind of cereal the children wanted. Wendy talks about how difficult that type of experience was for the children. They had experienced cataclysmic events, yet no one provided an opportunity for the children to own or talk about their feelings. The parents acted as if the episode had not even happened! These were some of the options open to the children: feel confused and wonder if the event really did happen or if they made it up; feel confused about the frustration, fear, and anger they felt and wonder if they were bad to feel what they feel; repress and/or deny their feelings.

Madeleine grew up knowing that an older brother had died before she was born. One day, at age eight, she asked Mother, "Did you cry when Frankie died?"

Mother answered, "Yes," but she shifted uncomfortably and looked away, then quickly changed the subject. Madeleine got the message: don't ask Mother about feelings.

When Cathleen Brooks was about eight years old, her father asked at the dinner table, "How was everyone's day?"

Cathleen immediately reported that she had an awful day. "A girl hit me on the playground, and I was really upset!" At that point, the father hit her younger brother who sat beside him. Cathleen said, "I got a distinct message: do not talk about my feelings. Something bad happens if you do."

Years later, she and her brother both became alcoholics. Both entered recovery, and she began working with ACAs. When speaking to a group, she told this incident. Afterward, she apologized to her brother. "I should have checked with you before telling that to an audience."

He said, "I'm glad you did that. All these years, I

thought I made that up." The father's behavior had been so inappropriate that the only way the son could handle it was to convince himself it was the result of his imagination.

### 3. Communication Is Often Indirect

Instead of communicating about thoughts and feelings, family members tend to communicate in ways that attempt to get them what they want without their having to risk asking for it. That would require them to take responsibility for their feelings and to make an active request. They lack the skills to do those two things. They, furthermore, are so afraid they will be turned down they don't risk disappointment and rejection by openly requesting.

Much victimization takes place within such a family system. Individuals blame others for what is wrong rather than taking personal responsibility for failed relationships and communications; people take out on others their feelings of hurt and anger rather than communicating and negotiating to get what they need and want.

### 4. Unrealistic Expectations

Some examples of this rule would be: be strong, be good, always be right, be perfect. Make us proud.

"The Smiths have always gone to college."

"In this family, we always do such-and-such."

"Oh, you never do such-and-such" (when a person has obviously just done exactly that).

"That just *isn't done*" (when the person has just done that).

"Of course, you know you did such-and-such" (when the person just said no, he didn't do that).

In these families, members are not valued for themselves. They are expected to fill roles. They do not get *being* messages that affirm them.

Labels are put onto family members, and they stop viewing each other as individuals but respond to labels and roles. "He's our smart child." "He's our dumb one." "She's our good one." "She's our problem." Two children can do the same thing, yet it is approved or disapproved according to stereotypes. The "good" child's messy room is ignored; the "bad" child gets reprimanded about her dirty room. Mother may show her anger more openly so she might be labeled in the minds of others as the angry one. Dad may be just as angry, or more so, but he suppresses his emotions and is viewed by the children and outsiders as the nice one.

Roles are important in these families. Members give each other many *ought* messages. "A husband ought to do such-and-such," "A woman's place, . . ." "Children should be seen and not heard, etc.," rather than viewing others as *human beings* with needs and feelings common to all people.

A child needs to receive subtle or direct affirmation messages from his parents that say, "I'm glad you're here." Even within the healthiest of families, where children are wanted and planned for, accidental pregnancies and births occur. In these homes, the children are never told that they were accidents. Within dysfunctional families, adult children report being told specifically by a parent, "You were an accident." In the alcoholic home, a parent might tell the child this while the parent is drunk, or the sober wife, in despair about her situation, may take out her feelings of rage on the child and report this inappropriate information to the child. This gives the child a strong *don't be* message that erodes the foundation of his self-esteem.

A child also needs to be told, "I'm glad you are who you are." In functional families, a couple (or one partner) might hope for a child of a certain sex, but when the baby arrives, the parents say, "We're just glad the baby is healthy, and we're glad we have what came." In dysfunctional families, children sometimes experience confusion about their sexual identities: females have received messages that they are not valued for being female, and males have received a similar message regarding their sexual identity.

At age eight, Ruth's friends came over to play. "Mike, what are you doing in a dress?" they asked. Ruth's mother learned that her daughter had identified herself as a boy to her peers and had always worn jeans and tee shirts before when playing. Her father is alcoholic.

Madeleine reports having felt a confusion about her role as a female.

> Dad's tape, when he got drunk, was to tell the daughters how terrible Mother was. "Don't be like your mother," he told us every weekend of our lives. Then who was I to be like? I didn't want to be like Daddy—intimidating, unkind, harsh, insensitive, selfish, impatient, high-tempered, and rejecting. Neither did I want to be like Mother—intimidated, powerless, controlled, passive, a victim, trapped.

Madeleine claimed her identify as a female but found it extremely difficult to relate to boys during her teenage dating years. She felt very shy, stiff, and fearful. She had difficulty choosing a marital partner. In a healthy family, a girl bases her idea of a future mate on what her father was like. Madeleine wound up marrying a passive, dependent man whom she took care of in the same way her mother took care of her alcoholic husband.

In her forties, Madeleine entered a support group composed of six men and one other woman. In that setting, she got in touch with the fact that she had "never sat comfortably in the chair of being female—I had always hovered above it, not fully claiming my identity. I had also viewed myself as a victim and had seen no benefits to being female." After that group experience, she sat firmly in the "female chair" and learned some of the benefits of being a woman.

Harriet was named that because her father wanted a boy whose name would have been Harry. Douglas (a female) was supposed to have been a boy. In many ways, individuals go through life knowing they were not fully accepted for who they are, especially when who they are was beyond their power to control. The message is: be something you're not, a decidedly unrealistic expectation.

Children are expected to take on roles and to execute behaviors far beyond their abilities. Kristen's alcoholic mother forced the twelve-year-old child to ride along while she drove from their upper-crust neighborhood to the sleazy side of town to buy liquor. "You watch to see if anybody is crossing the street. If I hit someone and kill him, it will be your fault." In her immaturity, Kristen believed her mother and took on the task of warning her mother when a pedestrian was in the path. Kristen can't explain her reasoning, but somehow she thought that when she got her own driver's license at sixteen her mother would release her from that duty. It didn't work out that way—she then required Kristen to drive on the liquor-buying trips.

## 5. Don't Be Selfish

In these homes, it is considered OK only to take care of others. Taking care of your own needs is viewed as doing something wrong. So ACAs try to feel good about themselves by taking care of others. Eventually their self-esteem becomes dependent on caretaking and they feel guilty if they do good things for themselves. And the mercury of their guilt breaks their emotional thermometers when they dare to put their own needs ahead of another's.

In time, the caretakers feel resentful toward those for whom they care because the recipients fail to recognize what the caretakers are doing for them. The caretakers then feel ashamed of their angry feelings and try to cover up by more caretaking. A further problem lies in the fact that caretakers often overhelp people, creating dependence, which is unhealthy. Because the helper feels comfortable only when others are leaning on him, the "helpee" accommodates the helper by remaining helpless.

A woman felt a victim in her household, feeling she had to take care of all the pets, force the children out of their beds to go to school each day and do other chores. She went away on a trip and feared the worst: nothing would take place during her absence. She returned to learn that the pets had been fed and the children had made it to school on time. The husband shrugged to his wife, "I know you'll supervise everything when you're here so I don't bother."

Eighty percent of the people in helping professions in the United States are ACAs. Those professions—social work, nursing, religious work, schoolteaching, the mental health field, and others—are usually characterized by long hours, low pay, and low recognition. Many ACAs have difficulty earning high pay for their work even though they are, as a group, extremely conscientious and deliver superior work.

A grandchild of an alcoholic considered entering a certain type of professional training. The interviewer, attempting to get the young woman to enroll in the program, promised her, "You'll make megabucks!" not realizing that would turn the woman off. If the interviewer had said, "You won't earn much money, but you can benefit mankind," the response might have been positive. That young woman could not believe herself worthy of wealth. (This is not to imply that people should not get involved in careers that benefit mankind.)

Cathleen Brooks says, "If we ever have a nuclear holocaust, I want to be between two ACAs because they will each grab me rather than protect themselves! They won't be concerned about their own safety, they'll be thinking about others!"

How can ACAs get out of this cycle of helping others excessively to the point of hurt to both parties? Getting a sense of personal worth enables individuals to recognize that it is OK to spend time, effort, and funds on their own well-being. This paradoxical motivation should appeal to caretakers. Other people grow and mature more by being given space to work out their problems by themselves; therefore, helping yourself, and not being as available for others as before, creates space for others to be helped the most!

One thing that helped me was to redefine the meaning of the word *help*. I had always thought helping meant to *do for* another. Through experience, I came to recognize that this came across as overprotecting and patronizing. It also involved invading another's space—I often helped when the other person had not asked me to. I wondered why my help often generated resentment rather than the expected appreciation. I came to see that it can be offensive to presume to help another. This implies a Mother-knows-best attitude that is resented. A cartoon showed a Boy Scout helping a protesting woman across the street who was saying, "But I don't want to cross the street!" I was the embodiment of that boy. When a person described a dilemma to me, I "hopped on my horse and galloped off" to solve the problem. Often, the person simply wanted me to listen, to understand, to give support.

Some people do not want their problems solved! They enjoy self-pity and resent attempts to remove the problem from their lives. A woman co-worker had a new problem (or a rehashing of a familiar one) every time she talked with me. I'd go into my rescuing act and throw responses: why not try this, why not try that? With a sigh, she would give a "Yes, but..." reply to each suggestion.

When I ran dry, she would smile a self-satisfied smile and say, "There's just no solution." I was slow catching on to the fact that she did not want help. I could have spared myself the emotional and physical energy and the effort that I put into trying to help her solve her problems.

When my husband and I were on the mission field, I exhausted myself helping people who did not want to be helped. A missionary couple stated that their son wanted to learn Hindi, the language of the East Indians living in that country. I assumed they meant they were looking for classes. They were new in the country, and I assumed they did not know where such classes were held. At that time we did not have a telephone, so I got into my car and made the rounds to locate a Hindi class. Now, remember, they did not ask me to. When I gave them the information, I learned they did not want the boy to study Hindi; they were afraid he would convert to the Hindu religion! That experience served as a turning point for me. I laughed heartily at myself and asked myself, "Is your life in order the way you want it to be?" A resounding *no* came back. So I decided to apply my energies where they were needed (and wanted) and to take care of my own responsibilities, which were many.

Only a well-cared-for machine, such as a car, can perform at peak level. Most people recognize that reality and take excellent care of their machines. The same is true for people: if caretakers are to truly help others, they must keep themselves in good condition, which calls for balance in their lives, something that is usually lacking in the lives of ACAs. They feel comfortable only when "on duty" and find it difficult to give recreation healthy space in their lives, in terms of allocating time and/or funds. In a conference on Caretakers Coping with Burnout, the leader gave a simple formula: to prevent burnout or to eradicate it, take good care of yourself. Identify things that you enjoy doing and give yourself permission to do them. The crux lies in the term *permission*. It is difficult for ACAs to give themselves permission to take time out for recreation and, heaven forbid, do nothing! once in a while.

Often when a person enters a support group or private counseling, she reports a few sessions later that she is making progress in being good to herself but is having severe guilt feelings about doing so. Our *shoulds* are so strong in our minds that when a person takes a baby step out of the caretaking position and does a little something purely for enjoyment, her guilt makes her feel as if she has gone "off the board." Group members (or the counselor) can give a realistic reading to the person; she is not taking a giant step into becoming selfish. With that encouragement, she can continue to move forward in creating balance within her life.

## 6. Do as I Say, Not as I Do

In the alcoholic home, this comes out as "Don't trust." This rule, perhaps more than any other, teaches us not to trust. If parents tell children to do one thing, then turn around and do the opposite, the children become confused and suspicious. ACAs report drunk fathers who drove down the highway at breakneck speed, frightening the family and laughing gleefully when the wife and children pleaded with him to stop. That same parent had strict rules about his children driving within the speed limit when he was sober.

The alcoholic is paranoid; he doesn't trust himself or others, and this distrustful way of relating spreads throughout the family system.

Parents may also promise to do something and then not follow through. Yet the child is told to keep promises. Alcoholics make promises when in a blackout that they don't remember later.

The alcoholic parent may tell the children he loves

them, but his behavior may be highly contradictory—
insensitive, selfish, even abusive. The children have trouble reconciling the two parts of the parent's personality.
Children start to wonder if parents love them and if the
children count. They stop taking risks and count only on
themselves.

## 7. It's Not OK to Play

Cathleen Brooks calls the alcoholic home a "war
zone." And people don't play in a foxhole with bullets
whizzing over their heads. The atmosphere in many alcoholic homes is calm in terms of the absence of violence,
but we must not discount the homes where the children
live in fear of bodily harm. Sometimes the terror comes
not directly from the parent but as a spinoff of the behavior of the parent. In Sue's home, her alcoholic mother was
the sole wage earner after her father left. The mother
worked sporadically and had poor skills for handling money. Bill collectors came frequently to the door. Her mother
worked in a tavern at night, and Sue stayed home alone.
One night, she climbed to look out the peephole when a
booming knock sounded on the door. The sheriff stood
there, shotgun in hand, demanding that Sue open the
door. Now in her thirties, she trembled and cried as she
recalled the incident. "I felt terrified!"

Co-Dependents believe that the world is a very serious place. They view life as difficult and painful. They
view themselves as unlovable, boring, stupid, ugly, and
wrong. Because of this, the Co-Dependent must work
twice as hard as everyone else just to feel OK. They come
to believe that what they *do* is who they *are,* so it becomes
increasingly important to their feeling OK that they not be
without something to do. They become addicted to work.

The longer people deny their need to play, the more
they suffer. Through play people discover who they are as
persons. But to play is to risk being spontaneous, and

perhaps even foolish, which is too scary for the Co-Dependent.

Think of what happened when you behaved spontaneously as a child. How many times did your parents laugh *with* you and everyone had a pleasurable moment? Were you laughed *at*? Were you made to feel foolish? Were you scolded? Were you blamed? For example, maybe you were told, "Now you've upset Daddy and he'll get drunk."

How often did your parents play with you? The alcoholic usually lives within a shell, isolated socially from his family and other people. It is rare for that parent to get down on the floor and play with a child or to plan an outing for the family. And family outings, intended to be fun, often end in misery for the other family members so nobody wants those events to continue.

In a TV film about an alcoholic father, the teenage daughters was scheduled to play in an orchestra concert at school. The family got dressed, and the father assembled the family for photos to commemorate the important occasion. Everyone joined in the high spirits, and the prognosis for the family having a congenial evening was good. Daddy was drinking heavily, though, and as the family got into the van to leave, something a child did caused the father to erupt hysterically and chaos resulted. The evening was ruined for all the other members of the family.

The unpredictability of the alcoholic's behavior inhibits spontaneity. The parent's response vacillates. Behavior that was approved one day brings a punishment the next, sometimes based on the parent's sobriety, sometimes on the impulsiveness of the alcoholic. Maybe Dad isn't drunk that day, but perhaps he has a horrible hangover and feels bad physically and feels guilty, so he explodes at a little thing the child does. Things are not constant in the child's life, and he does not have the guarantee that "If I do this, Daddy or Mommy will respond in this way. . . ." The child never knows, so it is safer not to test the waters. The child may deliberately do something designed to bring praise, and to his surprise, it brings a rebuke. Madeleine, at twelve, burst out at the end of a supper everyone had agreed was unusually good, "Mother's the best cook in the whole world!"

"Pshaw!" huffed Dad, the alcoholic. A child's compliment to the mother was labeled worthy of a criticism! Dad felt jealous of the children's loyalty to Mother, so he had to put down any indication that revealed the child's approval of Mother.

# Some Dysfunctional Communication Styles

The basic formula for effective interpersonal communication is very simple. God gave us mouths to talk to each other and eyes to look at each other while talking. He made us feeling beings, so we can relate to other people on an emotional level. He did not give us the ability to know what another person is thinking and feeling, so it is necessary for two individuals to let each other know what is going on within them. When two people look at one another directly and talk out their feelings, effective communication can result.

That type of effective communication rarely takes place. Few parents know how to communicate that way, which means that children (who then become marital partners and parents in a new home) do not learn how to relate person-to-person. Thus, the dysfunctional styles continue from generation to generation.

Here are some dysfunctional styles of communicating. Most of these are found in an alcoholic home.

## 1. Talk *at*, Not *to* a Person

What does it mean to talk at a person? Here are some examples.

*Make a speech at a person rather than share your*

*feelings*. For example, "When I was your age, I did thus-and-so. . . ." A person may speak calmly and reasonably— he may not yell or act angrily—but he does not link up with the other person emotionally.

Naomi said to her husband, "I'm feeling a lot of pain in our marriage."

Dan, who majored in philosophy in college, answered, "Pain is a part of life."

"What does that have to do with us?"

"We need to accept the fact that pain is everywhere and not let it bother us." In no way did he connect with her emotionally, he stuck to the topic of pain. Rather than tell her how he felt, he made a patient, patronizing speech about pain being a part of life and that people throughout history have experienced pain. The underlying messages were: since pain is a part of life, you should not complain about having pain; telling me about your pain in our marriage threatens me, so I will distance you (and my own feelings) by making a speech about the inanimate subject of pain; when you let me know you're unhappy with me, I feel helpless and frightened, so one way I can gain a feeling of control is to make an intellectual speech; because your expressions of unhappiness make me feel uncomfortable, I'm going to do whatever I can to get you to stop talking about it; since pain is a part of life, don't try to do anything about the pain in our marriage—let's just passively submit to whatever pain comes along.

Sally, fifty-two, had gained the courage to divorce her alcoholic husband of thirty-one years. She felt the need to talk with him heart-to-heart before leaving. He opened each day by drinking beer. Sally knew that after two beers he would not be available for any meaningful exchange, so she approached him early one Sunday morning when he was not going to go to work. "Where did our marriage go wrong?" she asked.

He proceeded to make a speech on the topic of,

"Husbands and wives should respect one another." At no point did he talk about *their* marriage.

*Make rigid demands without respect for feelings.* One person says, "This is the way it's going to be," without asking for any input from the other or without asking how the other feels about it; giving orders, talking top-down rather than person-to-person. "Now, listen to me, young man. As long as you put your feet under my table, you'll do as I say. . . ."

*Use an intimidating tone of voice.* The tone of voice is important in effective communication. Words seen in print could seem free of any intimidation or threat, but the tone of voice could change the meaning completely. The words "Come here" could have varied meaning, and varied responses from the hearer, according to tone of voice.

## 2. Talk *About*, Not *to* People

Person A talks to Person B about Person C: the classic triangle. Person A may have strong feelings of hostility toward Person C, but she or he never knows about it. Person A may tell everyone except Person C. Why is this? We don't know how to sit down quietly, look another person in the eye and say, "I felt offended by what you did." We also fear (in fact, we know) that the only way the other person could possibly respond to us would be to get angry. We fear anger, so we withhold our feelings from that person. We make assumptions about why that person did the offensive act and never give the person an opportunity to clarify what he did, forgetting that only that person can let us know what he felt and why he behaved as he did. Perhaps the few times · we did attempt to communicate to another in a direct way ended disastrously so we don't have the courage to do it again.

Parents may lie awake all night talking about the delinquent behavior of a teenage child without ever talking to the child herself. One husband told his dog about his anger toward his wife! When his wife would say, "I'm sure Ruff isn't interested in the fact that you are angry with me—how about telling me?" the husband would answer, "Oh, can't you take a joke?" He also talked to his newspaper about his anger toward his wife.

She would lower the paper and say, "Tell me what you're feeling." Again, he would brush her aside as if she were making something out of nothing. He finally resolved the problem by moving to another state. (He took the dog with him.)

Gossip is talking *about* rather than talking *to*. Friendships have been broken and reputations ruined by gossip. Individuals felt hurt by the actions of another but no one talked *to* anyone.

### 3. Little Eye Contact

We start to feel shy when we look directly at another person. Confrontation, especially, can be threatening, so it is easier to look somewhere else when telling someone we are unhappy about something he did. Some people do their most effective "communicating" over the telephone. They can come across as firm, authoritative, in control, intimate when they are speaking to an instrument. When faced with a person, they become tongue-tied. Some people can express affection and share intimately better over the telephone because they feel a safe distance from the hearer.

Sally and her alcoholic husband communicated completely by notes or by telephone. They called each other during the day from their respective work settings and left notes at home before going out.

A woman who attended one of my workshops said, "When I started dating my husband, I actually thought his eyes were set in his head sideways! He could not look anyone in the eye. After I met his family, I saw that no one looked at anyone else when speaking."

Start observing the lack of eye contact between individuals. A husband and wife often communicate at the end of the day from room to room, over the shoulder, from behind a newspaper, while watching TV. A wife, standing at the sink peeling potatoes, throws over her shoulder, "How was your day?"

The husband responds from another room, "Fine! How was yours?" He may even be reading the newspaper and watching TV at the same time!

Sometimes a couple has wonderful sharing in bed after the lights are out; but all day long, when they could look at each other, not much communication takes place. The darkness gives anonymity and protection. Madeleine said, "I began to wonder why my husband and I had such good sharing when we went on vacations and it didn't last when we came home. Then I realized that those talks took place when we were in the car—he was talking to the windshield and I was talking to the side of his head!"

## 4. Send Messages Through a Third Person

This is similar to a triangle—two people talk to each other and a third is excluded, except that no message is sent to the third party.

Children may ask Mother, "Will you ask Daddy if we can do such-and-such?" Mother serves as the buffer between Daddy and the children. Unless the father is physically abusive, it is better if Mother can refuse to get in between the children and their father. When Mother does act as a buffer, it reinforces in the children's minds the idea that Daddy is a monster. If the children deal directly with him, they might find that he responds differently toward them than he does toward Mother (or how Mother perceives him to be). Children need to learn to deal with their parents, even when the parents are difficult and unreasonable. When one parent serves as a buffer, the children are dealing with the reality (that the other parent is difficult) and with Mother's protective behavior, which amplifies the father's faults. The children need to learn to deal with difficult authority figures—they may (most assuredly, will!) encounter them later in their marriages, their work, their churches, and elsewhere. In dealing with that parent, the children might learn skills for coping and might discover a side of the parent he had never revealed as a spouse.

Since the mother probably had an intimidating parent, it is easy for her to overidentify with the children and to project her own feelings onto the situation, exaggerating their victimized state, encouraging their feelings of self-pity and their feelings of powerlessness. It would be better if she would support the children in developing a direct relationship with their father. They might get fewer permissions to do things, but they might have a healthier relationship with their father and might gain skills important for coping in life.

## 5. Secrecy Rather than Openness

In these homes is heard, "Don't show Daddy my report card because it's so bad."

"OK, Son, I won't."

"Sh-h-h! Here comes your daddy (or mother)."

"Don't tell your mother (or daddy) this."

A mother discovered drugs in her son's sock in the laundry hamper. When she confronted him, he lied, "It isn't mine, it belongs to my friend. I knew he would get into trouble with his parents if he kept it. . . . And, Mom, don't tell Dad, OK?" She didn't and learned along the way that the drugs belonged to her son who was into heavy drug use. The family entered a rehabilitation program and the mother learned that her protection of her children contributed a great deal to the son's drug problem.

Events are kept from family members. An adult may learn that an uncle committed suicide, that a relative had an out-of-wedlock child, or that he was adopted. ACAs have learned at their father's funeral that he had been married and divorced prior to being married to their mother. They meet stepsiblings whom they never knew existed. Rather than everyone and his behavior being accepted and laid out on the table for everyone to know about, these people keep secrets about each other.

## 6. Confusing Messages

Double-bind communication was discovered when psychiatrists were studying why schizophrenic patients who began to get well in the hospital regressed when they went home or had contact with their families. The main conclusions drawn from the study was that one of the primary causes of schizophrenia is double-bind communication: a parent says one thing while doing the opposite. It is impossible for the child to please—while doing one thing, he disobeys the other. The textbook case told about a patient whose mother was coming to visit him. As the two approached each other in the hall, he reached out to embrace her. He saw her body stiffen in anticipation, so he dropped his arms. "What's the matter?" she chided, "don't you want to hug your mother?"

Alcoholics are very needy people emotionally, yet they can't handle emotional intimacy. One message the children receive is, "Come close—go away." ACAs find themselves with a contradictory need to be close but feeling uncomfortable with closeness.

Estelle and Gary, both ACAs, had dated for some months and were considering getting married. She began to have doubts, however. Whenever she responded to his invitation (often subtle) to get close emotionally, they would have a satisfying exchange. Then he would say something cruel. "We have a hug-and-hit relationship," she said.

ACAs often feel lonely and isolated from other human

beings. Others may view them as friendly, outgoing, kind, etc., yet many have unsatisfactory social and intimate relationships.

## 7. No Answers to Questions or Inadequate Explanations

Cathleen Brooks's father often fell asleep, drunk, on the garage floor when he came home from work. The younger children would ask, "Why is Daddy sleeping on the garage floor?"

Cathleen would answer, "Well, Daddy works very hard and he is very tired, so he falls asleep before he can get into the house."

Children may be told, "Be quiet so you won't upset Daddy and then he'll drink." No explanation is given as to why noise upsets Daddy or why he handles his upset state by drinking.

The alcoholic may change his behavior without explanation. Cathleen Brooks gives this example out of her home. The parents announced happily one night, "We're going to the movies!" The children scurried around getting ready. By the time they gathered in the living room, something had happened to change the parents' minds. The children were given no explanation, and when one asked, the father snapped, "We're not going."

When a child whined, "But I want to go," the father said sternly, "We are the parents here, and we make the decisions. We're not going to the movies."

A child may ask about something that is going on, and the sober parent may whisper, "Just don't ask."

Naomi, an ACA parent, found that she gave many contradictory messages to her children. Because Naomi's background was so restrictive and she was always told no, she found herself unable to say no to her children. On the other hand, she moved in a professional, peer, and religious setting that called for children to obey very strictly.

Naomi handled the situation by allowing the children to do something forbidden, then scolded them for it. Thus she satisfied the two parts of herself.

## 8. Passive Communication

I read this insightful statement: "When your teenager isn't talking, he's telling you something." Whenever anyone of any age doesn't talk, he is telling the others in his life something important. *Not talking* is one of the ways of communicating passively rather than directly. Others are:

*Hinting.* A wife wants her husband to read a book, so she lays it on the coffee table, hoping he will spot it and read it. She doesn't tell him directly what she wants—that would probably cause him to get on the defensive, and then he would definitely not read the book. The communication between them would be healthier, though, and the relationship would be advanced more than if the man read the book.

*Pouting.* A young couple told me that their three-and-a-half-year-old daughter had started pushing out her bottom lip when she didn't like something that happened. Their inclination was to punish her so she would stop doing it. "That is telling you that something is going on within her on the feeling level," I said. "Rather than approach the matter from the authoritarian point of view, how about saying to her, 'When you push out your lip, that lets me know that something is bothering you. Can you tell me what it is?'" Often parents' first instinct is to quell what they view as rebellious behavior. It is healthier to explore with the child the feelings behind the behavior. This says to the child that it is OK to have feelings and that it is OK to talk about them. The problem behavior usually goes away.

*Denying that anything is wrong when asked.* "You've been awfully quiet all evening, is something wrong?"

"Oh, no," said with meaningful facial expressions of martyrdom and annoyance.

*Stopping speaking.*

*Assuming the other person will read one's mind and taking no responsibility for informing the other.* Dan, son of a hypochondriac mother who demanded to know his every thought (so he concluded she could read his mind), married Naomi, an ACA, whose alcoholic father had hinted rather than given direct orders to the children. Naomi hinted and felt angry when her signals were not picked up and accused Dan of not being an alert person. She would say, "I thought you could tell when I did that that I meant such-and-such."

Dan would get upset about the way she did something. When she would ask him why he hadn't told her what he wanted or how he felt about something, he would say, "I thought you could read my mind."

*Glaring.*

*Sighing.* Sighing is a nonverbal way of expressing unhappiness, frustration, or inner weariness.

*Forgetfulness.* One wife "forgot" to salt the food every night. Her husband was angry every night. She genuinely apologized because she did not consciously forget. When I used this example in a workshop, a young woman said, "That was my mother! Only she knew that she might have forgotten, so just before putting the food on the table, she would salt it just to be sure. So, the food was usually salted twice!"

*Tardiness.*

## 9. Acting Out

I once asked a man who had been married sixteen years (happily, so far as I could tell), "Without telling me the incident, think back to the first time your wife got mad at you when you were first married." He nodded, indicating he had a memory in mind. "How did you know she was mad? Did she tell you?" He shook his head. "You just knew, didn't you?" He nodded agreement. "Now, think back to the first time you got mad at her." After a pause, he nodded. "How did she know? Did you tell her?" Again, he shook his head.

We rarely tell someone else we are angry: we show it. And those close to us get very adept at reading the clues we give out, just as we become skilled at reading their clues.

Acting out anger includes slamming doors, throwing things, and the like. "She really knows I'm mad!" Yes, but why didn't you tell her?

A teenager who gets into drugs, gets pregnant, or runs away from home is often acting out his or her feelings of hurt and anger.

Here is a hypothetical example. A man comes home from work greatly dejected. He learned that day that he will not get the promotion he had hoped for. His self-esteem is suffering, and he needs the company and comfort of his wife. When he gets home, he learns that she plans to go out for a monthly get-together with some women friends. Rather than ask his wife outright to stay home with him because he needs her (for fear she might reveal that she preferred to be with her friends that evening), he asks her why doesn't she stay home and attacks her "hen parties." She becomes defensive and goes out, stinging from his remarks. Can you think of an episode you had with some member of your family or a friends that resembles that example?

## 10. Repetitious Conversation

People in these families tend, for several reasons, to say the same things over and over. Individuals get locked into certain roles which govern what they say. Members are afraid to rock the boat, so they say what they have learned keeps everything under control. The lack of spontaneity in these homes means that it is not safe for one to behave differently. The rule of silence means that people keep on saying accepted things.

Naomi found that she repeated herself to Dan because he didn't listen well and often did not hear what she said, and his anxieties filled his mind to such an extent that he had difficulty remembering what he did hear. Consequently, Naomi would characteristically think, *I know I told him this Tuesday, but how knows if he heard or remembered?* So she would tell the same story over.

When she scolded him for not listening to her, he said, "But you repeat yourself so much." A real cycle was in operation.

## Guidelines for Functional Communication

1. Talk to the person.
2. Use direct eye contact.
3. Be open.
4. Answer questions directly and give explanations.
5. Say what you feel rather than acting it out.
6. Share your feelings rather than giving *should* messages.

Here is the basic formula for effective communication: Make "I feel..." statements, then make a request. Often the request is simply, "Please listen," or "Please understand me." Sometimes the person needs to make a specific request, such as, "I want you to stay home with me tonight instead of going out as you had planned."

Earlene agreed with her sixteen-year-old son that when he made all *B*s on his report card for two semesters she would get him a car and named the amount she could pay. His grades did not improve, and she felt fearful that he was going to fail his courses in school so she gave him *should* messages: "You should study more and you shouldn't spend so much time with your friends and watching TV." The son is an intelligent person and knows the score. He knows he should study more if he is to pass his courses. One dynamic that is taking place, though, is that he is struggling to gain more control over his own life and to be more free from parental injunctions. The more Earlene pressed Ray, the more he resisted studying, and his grades continued to move on a downward spiral. Earlene felt even more fearful and gave more *should* messages. The tension between the two escalated.

I worked with Earlene about sharing her feelings with her son rather than trying to control his behavior and to allow him the freedom to make a choice and live with the consequences. She said, "Ray, I'm feeling frightened about your grades because it upsets me to think you will fail and have to repeat this semester. You are intelligent and I know you are capable of making good grades, and I would like for you to. According to state law, you cannot be required to go to school, so your attendance and your grades are up to you. I just want you to know how I feel about it." Ray was exposed to a vital lesson about human communication and his subsequent behavior showed he had better feelings about his mother. He also had the opportunity to do some growing. Those lessons are just as important as grades.

Earlene has made progress in sharing her feelings with Ray and she has said, "Now, when we eat dinner, he tells me about his life. We don't fight anymore." When a friend drove his new car over to show Ray, he looked dejected as they walked back into the apartment. Earlene patted him on the shoulder and said, "I know it's hard for you when your friends have cars and you don't." It is now up to him to earn the grades if he wants the car.

The *request is not a demand*. When people first learn to make direct requests, their usual expectation is that the other person must grant it. If that doesn't happen, the asker feels let down and angry. Jill works as a waitress and has allowed others to walk all over her all of her life. She has started to take up for herself and has told another waitress, "I just want you to know I felt angry when you did such-and-such today." The girl simply shrugged and walked off. Jill reported to her support group that she felt angry at the girl's response—she had expected the girl to say, "Oh, I'm sorry." We reminded her that the girl was under no obligation to apologize— she might even have taken offense at Jill's expression of anger. The important thing was that Jill communicated her feelings directly and spontaneously, which enhanced her personal growth.

Communicating directly is a healthy style which creates space for the other person to respond in a similar manner. It does not guarantee that the hearer will respond that way for two reasons. First, so few people have received "I feel..." statements, they do not know how to respond in the same vein. People have usually been delivered "You" statements (accusations) all their lives, so an "I feel..." statement is usually heard as an accusation, even when none was made.

Jeanne, subject of the chapter "Forgiving the Sober Parent," granted me an interview and I wrote the article on my word processor. I invited her over to look at it and approve it before printing it. We sat side by side at the screen. At a certain point, she said, "I don't feel comfortable with that."

I stiffened defensively because what I heard was, "You've done it wrong and I'm mad at you."

In my mind, I responded, "I just wrote what you told me!" It took several seconds for my anxieties to settle so that I recognized what she had actually said. She then explained that when she gave the interview, she didn't realize how that experience would look in print. Seeing it in words made her feel uncomfortable and that was exactly what she was sharing—how she felt. We then worked on the sentences until she felt comfortable with the material.

A woman friend, an ACA, has a habit of blurting out impulsive statements. One day, I told her on the phone about something I was doing. She instantly replied, "You're selfish!" I allowed her to catch me up in defending myself. She then proceeded to tell me how to do it her way.

I felt uncomfortable about the way the conversation was going, so I said quietly and firmly, "Juanita, I want you to know I don't like to be called selfish."

She retorted, "Now I'm angry!"

"Why are you angry?" I asked.

"I am very angry," she repeated and soon ended the conversation.

When we met for lunch the next week, I brought up the incident. "Sara, you were livid," she said dramatically. To me, livid implies red in the face, enraged, out of control. I emphasized that I had spoken quietly and that I was fully in control of my emotions and my behavior at the time. She held onto her position about how I had spoken. This is a good example of how ACAs feel so threatened by any hint of anger or rejection that we exaggerate it and do not literally hear correctly what the other person says when that person gives us an "I feel..." statement.

Dot, a young professional woman in one of my support groups, became excited about communicating more directly to other people. She brought this incident for our evaluation one night. She was having dinner with a girl friend and her boyfriend who was throwing croutons at

Dot across the table. She said, "I don't like people to throw things at me." The girl friend rebuked Dot later, saying that she was becoming obnoxious by being so outspoken with her friends. The group supported Dot's behavior and helped her understand that although she didn't rebuke the young man he felt rebuked and his overprotective girl friend, in turn, rebuked Dot. The only way she could have escaped being labeled obnoxious would have been to passively let the young man throw things at her.

Rather than demanding that the other person grant your requests, you are free to make choices following denials. Clara, an ACA, is married to Al, also an ACA. Whenever she makes a direct request of him, his fear of being controlled causes him to deny it. Clara must make a choice about whether to stay married to a man who tells her at every turn that he will not do anything she wants.

The second reason people usually don't respond to "I feel..." messages is that they have never learned to do so. Dealing in feelings makes many people feel uncomfortable so they try to turn the conversation in a different direction.

The average communication between two persons has two exchanges if one person gets better and starts communicating in a new way. The first person initiates a conversation with an "I feel..." statement or a statement inviting the other person to share feelings, or the first person confronts the other. The second person usually responds with a controlling, discounting statement. "Oh, you ought to stop analyzing everything so much! Just forget your feelings and get on with your life." This is an attempt to intimidate. In the past, the first person backed off and the exchange ended. When an individual starts getting healthier, he persists beyond the intimidating answer and tries to get the second person to join him in having a satisfying exchange.

The following quiz is on co-dependent rules. The left side of the page lists those and the right side of the page lists healthy rules. Score yourself from one to five according to where you view yourself now. This is a good quiz to take every few months to chart your progress.

| Co-Dependency Rules | | | | | Growth-Enhancing Rules |
|---|---|---|---|---|---|
| 1. It's not okay to talk about problems. | 1 | 2 | 3 | 4 | 5 I try to share my problems and get feedback about myself from others. |
| 2. Feelings should not be expressed openly. | 1 | 2 | 3 | 4 | 5 I try to express any persistent feeling with the appropriate person. |
| 3. Communication is indirect, using "messengers." | 1 | 2 | 3 | 4 | 5 I speak for myself directly to whomever is appropriate for the message. |
| 4. Unrealistic expectations. | 1 | 2 | 3 | 4 | 5 I am learning to let go of perfection, details, and being "right" all the time. |
| 5. Don't be selfish (guilt). | 1 | 2 | 3 | 4 | 5 Doing things just for me is healthy. I am to enjoy caring for me. |
| 6. Do as I say, not as I do. | 1 | 2 | 3 | 4 | 5 I try to follow through with actions rather than just words. |
| 7. It's not okay to play. | 1 | 2 | 3 | 4 | 5 I let myself have fun. I can even be silly sometimes. |
| 8. Don't rock the boat. | 1 | 2 | 3 | 4 | 5 I am learning to look at change as healthy, as fun, as a challenge. |

# 5

# Marital Styles of
# Adult Children of Alcoholics

In the alcoholic marriage, the name of the game is emotional distancing. The bottle serves the purpose of keeping the couple apart. In marriages of ACAs, the same need to keep the partner at a distance is in operation. If drinking is not present, then conflict, often over the children, serves the purpose that the bottle does in the original home. When individuals begin to feel close to another person, one technique used to push the person away is to start finding fault with the other. That justifies the distancing on the rational level. The person is unaware of the real reason he must put distance between himself and his spouse. ACAs use many other tactics to bring about the root need in the marriage—to prevent emotional closeness.

This fear of emotional intimacy can go into operation immediately following the wedding ceremony. One man told his counselor that as he walked down the aisle to meet his bride, he was thinking of how much he loved her and wanted to be married to her. As the couple walked out of the church, he thought, *I don't love her and don't want to be married to her.* As he escorted his new wife into the car he said, "Shut up and don't say a word." This man was unprepared for the impact the ceremony itself could have on him.

When Shirley, a new client, told me about the severe problems in her marriage, I asked when it had started falling apart. "The day after the wedding," she answered. Her husband, a forty-year-old bachelor, began to say that he was too old for marriage and began to retreat.

Roberta, a successful career woman who manages a three million-dollar budget for a medical facility, is married to a man who is equally successful in his career. "We are unable to handle emotional intimacy," she reports. "We relate completely around each being proud of the other's work. My husband acts very loving toward me when we are at church and people there think of us as an ideal couple, but when we are at home at the same time, we are always in separate rooms. We don't quarrel, but it is too threatening to each of us to be alone together." The only time they talk is when one of the children does something wrong. Then each blames the other with, "Why didn't you teach him not to do that?" The other says, "But, I thought you did."

## Workaholism in the Marriage

Workaholism serves the purpose of keeping marriage partners apart. Frank, greatly in need of emotional warmth, married Alice, who had much warmth and gave it freely. Frank thought that would feel awfully good. After a while, Frank, unaccustomed to handling warmth and closeness, got a second job "to take care of our financial strain," which kept him gone from home nearly all of his wife's waking hours. He had no awareness of his true motives, only of his discomfort. Alice, who couldn't live without closeness and warmth, divorced the absent Frank.

# Projection of Parents onto Spouses

ACAs can project their parents onto their spouses. For example, the husband may be an excellent partner, but if the wife had a hurtful experience with her father, she may "put the face of her father" onto her husband, and respond to his supposed acts in the same way she responded to her father. One tiny complaint from the husband can be viewed as a brutal attack by the wife and she can counter-attack, escalating the exchange into a full-blown conflict, especially if the husband reacts in kind. Out of the wife's background of being intimidated, the situation could go in the opposite direction—she could feel abused but back off and swallow her resentment. The husband may have no idea (in fact, has no way of knowing) how his action or communication impacted on his wife. She stockpiles her resentments and may act them out or may blow up period-ically, which does not communicate to her spouse how she feels in a way that he can understand or respond to in any constructive way. The same thing, of course, can happen from husband to wife. Both may be doing this at the same time, which means that the marriage is being slowly killed.

Until the individuals effectively work through their resentments and other feelings toward their parents, much projecting may occur. One expert in the family systems theory of counseling says, "Sketch your family tree on a piece of paper, going back to include all of the ancestors you knew personally. Then draw a line separating yourself from any of the persons with whom you are currently having problems—especially your spouse and your chil-dren. Go back up to the previous generations, especially your parents, and work through any unresolved problems there." He promises that the problems on the current level will start working out.

Why does he make such a claim? For one thing, when you gain the courage to communicate with, and perhaps confront, your parents, you can then behave with more courage with your own family. Passiveness starts to fade. When you talk with your parents, you will undoubtedly learn information that will surprise you, which can clear up gray areas in your own perceptions. You may be able to let go of some anger you have held for years when you find out how your parent actually felt (not how you thought he or she felt). The greater closeness you will have after resolving problems will change you as a person, and you will be a different person within your present family. You will perhaps feel more comfortable with closeness in general. You may gain greater insight into why your spouse or children are angry with you. Maybe you have been behaving toward them in the same way the parent behaved toward you, which caused your angry response.

Ken, disgusted because his mother responded to his father's alcoholism with hypochrondria, finds himself unable to show any sympathy or caring on the rare occasions when his wife, a remarkably healthy woman, gets sick. He not only offers no help but also gets angry and attacks her verbally and abandons her, emotionally and literally. "Are you really sick?" he first accuses, sarcastically. Since Ken perceived that his mother's illnesses were fabricated to gain attention from the family members and control of the family, he projects his mother onto all women—whenever a woman gets sick, she can't possibly be really sick. Marty assures him she really is sick, so Ken, propelled back into the feelings he had as a son (where he especially felt unable to express himself openly), stalks out of the bedroom, thrusting cruelly, "Well, if you insist on being sick, then do it all by yourself!" He does not offer to make her a cup of tea or to get a cold cloth for her forehead—those thoughtful things that may have little medicinal value but which aid tremendously in recovery. He communicates his disgust at her for "daring to get sick!"

## Perfectionism in Marriage

Since perfectionism exists in the alcoholic home, ACAs carry this quality into their marriages. They can have excessively high ideals about what their marriages should be, acting out the characteristics of the home which call for unrealistic expectations. Since they lack the skills to bring about a marriage on such a level, they set themselves up for failure. This leads to each blaming the other for what is happening.

In addition to having unrealistic ideals for the marriage itself, the partner could have those expectations for his own participation in the marriage that set him up for disappointment and failure. He can behave in the relationship according to what he thinks he ought to do rather than act out of his own feelings.

## Avoidance in Marriage

Avoidance is a frequent style in these marriages. "When I dated my husband," Lynn said, "he was a camera buff. I used to think, *If I could just get that camera away from around his neck, we might have some direct communication.* Now, he spends every moment at home in front of his shortwave radio. I've stopped blaming his hobbies—I see he will do anything to avoid me." He tunes her out, physically, the way he did his mother. Lynn is constantly amazed to learn that he did not actually hear something she said, which gives her tremendous frustration.

Amanda's husband retreats behind a book each evening, Ella's buries himself in the computer, and Charlotte's husband flees to the garden. Individuals can not only avoid each other but also avoid conflict and tasks.

# Influences on Choice of Partner

Coming out of an alcoholic home influences the choice of marital partner. Many ACAs marry alcoholics. One study showed that as high as 60 percent of daughters of alcoholic fathers married alcoholic men. "Why, in heaven's name?" you well might ask. "Didn't she learn from her own experience how awful that can be?"

Several reasons are suggested for this behavior. This is normal for the daughter. It doesn't occur to her that other options exist. This may be a way for her to feel close to her father. This may be a way of identifying with her mother.

She may not have recognized the suitor's drinking pattern as being that of a problem drinker. Maybe her father was a binge drinker and this man drinks a little bit every day. She may not recognize the potential for alcoholism. The drinking may not have started when she dated and married him.

The woman may marry a man who is addicted to drugs or work, but she may have her eye fixed so intensely on spotting alcoholism that she may fall into a hole nearly as bad, though with a different label. Her low self-esteem may tell her she is not worthy of anything better.

Sally observed her alcoholic father's doing things such as coming into the backyard on a hot afternoon and dousing his head under the outdoor faucet. That didn't seem to her to be unusual; didn't all fathers do that? She was married to an alcoholic husband for fifteen years and didn't know it until she read a list of the symptoms in a newspaper article. She thought that was the way all men behaved.

Sally loved two alcoholics in her lifetime. She learned that her first teenage crush died of alcoholism in his thirties. She married Jake, an extremely handsome young man. While his drinking began and increased, she grew in her career, becoming a vice-president of a bank. During some of the years, she supported Jake while he either went to school (completing his BA and his MA degrees) or was unemployed but not going to school. After sixteen years, she divorced him because of the drinking. He stopped, and because she loved him, she remarried him.

The drinking resumed. It took Sally fifteen more years, thirty-one years after the original marriage, to make a final break. Her husband's final appeal to her, a satisfying sex life, stopped abruptly when their only child left home, after twenty-six years of marriage. Perhaps the daughter had served as a buffer to protect him from feeling too close to his wife, but when he cut off the only act of relating to her, she moved into the guest room. She finally concluded, after several years of therapy, that she deserved better than that and divorced Jake. Due to his physical and emotional health, however, she agreed to move out of the house (that she had paid for over the years) and take an apartment. She experienced much grief over the loss of her house because she had created an expression of her self in the way she decorated it. She finally made a break, but was self-sacrificing to the end.

If ACAs marry nondrinking people, they usually choose dependent types. The partner may use no drugs of any kind, but the dynamics of the alcoholic marriage are carried out. The spouse is the Dependent, the ACA is the Co-Dependent, finding herself acting in identical ways to her mother who was married to the alcoholic.

The ACA spouse can find herself doing the same accommodating; feeling as if everything is her fault; agreeing to carry all the responsibility to relieve the dependent spouse who is easily threatened by responsibility; raising the children because the partner doesn't see that as part of his job; tolerating verbal and emotional abuse; tolerating rejection and assuming something is wrong with her; covering up for him in work, in social situations, and with the children; working to support him during times of unemployment; staying during years of depression and/or other emotional or physical illnesses; staying in a marriage that is empty and unsatisfying in general.

Anita married a man with a hereditary heart problem. He abused his condition by smoking heavily and refused to do the exercises prescribed by his physician. He took no share in helping to raise the children nor in meeting her emotional needs, yet made himself constantly available to do errands and repair jobs for his parents. Anita advanced in her career, and when she reached a level of financial ability to support herself and the children, she gained the courage to decide to divorce Ed. Before she could actually tell him, he lost his job. She became depressed and said, "I can't divorce him now because he can't support himself." Eventually, she moved to the point where she recognized it was not her responsibility to support a dependent husband who took little responsibility for himself and proceeded with the divorce.

Matt married Edna, an inefficient young woman who seemed unable to "get herself together." He was an overachiever who reached executive status in his work, and it was not necessary for her to work. Even with few outside responsibilities, she could not accomplish the tasks of grocery shopping, meal preparation, house cleaning, and laundry. Executive Matt would come home in the evenings, take a cold, leftover casserole out of the refrigerator and eat out of the dish—his complete dinner. When the two children came along, he took on the jobs of bathing the girls, supervising their homework, correcting their English, and enrolling them in Girl Scouts. Any increase in pressure on Edna caused her to explode irrationally. After each episode, she acted as if nothing had happened. Matt tolerated this behavior passively. He justified staying in the marriage because of the children and because of his own poor physical health.

Matt's situation is an example of another phenomenon in the ACA marriage. Individuals who got a message in their homes, "You must not leave," and who observed their sober parents staying in the face of the intolerable, often feel unable to leave a bad marriage.

## Sexual Dysfunctioning

Sexual dysfunctioning can take place in these marriages. Each partner can express his/her anger through the sexual relationship. The wife may become nonorgasmic. She may continue to participate in the sex act but make only her body available. When a person makes love with another person outside of love, that person becomes split. The wife struggles with the need to value herself and her feelings that she must meet her husband's needs, even at her own expense. She can then act out her anger toward him (and herself) in various ways. Her sense of splitness can have serious effects on her emotional health.

In the case of the man, he could become impotent. He may, though, continue to be able to function normally but feels his wife's withdrawal and lack of participation. This has great effects on his self-esteem and he can feel inadequate as a lover and as a man. He, then, will act out his anger in various ways. As theorized in Jake's case, because the sex act is the ultimate in closeness and trusting, the partner may be unable to participate.

ACAs are often immature and the wife may view herself as a child rather than as a woman and may actually be a child in a woman's body. She may not be in touch with her own sexual feelings, or she may feel guilty for having those feelings (as she did when she was younger) and for having sex itself. She may be unable to claim her sexual identity as an adult. Ethel's husband wanted her to wear sexy nightgowns but she felt she should buy modest ones so that if the children saw the gowns in the laundry they wouldn't see plunging necklines and revealing styles. Ethel viewed herself as being responsible for meeting her husband's sexual needs but had no concept of her own needs for sexual satisfaction. She "delivered" sex to her husband in a Victorian sense as that being her "wifely duty."

Often, the children in the alcoholic home do not see the parents exchanging spontaneous, genuine physical affection. The adult children can feel that being romantic or giving time to sex is silly or as a waste of time. They may work until it is so late at night that they are tired, or they do not schedule time for sex nor allot money to getting away for a night at a hotel or doing something similar to acknowledge their legitimate need for sexual pleasure.

Wade was in touch with his own sex needs and was able to claim them within the marriage, but he was such a boy in relationship to his parents (especially his mother) and the world that he behaved in a split manner. He actively enjoyed having sex with his wife, but outside of the bedroom, he acted, in his wife's words "like a eunuch." He pressured her to wear loose-fitting clothing that would in no way show that she had a very good figure. He even accused her of flaunting her figure when she actually had a modest dress code. She once accused, "The only thing I could wear that would make you feel comfortable would be a nun's habit." With peers, Wade acted like a prude and a goody-goody.

Wade had never made the healthy cut of the tie between himself and his mother. So much of his behavior was designed, unconsciously, to say to his mother, "I really have not taken another woman before you. You are still number one with me." He was also so immature that he could not claim his place in society as a man, and doing that would include acknowledging himself as a sexual being who incorporated sexual behavior into his life. He viewed himself as a boy and related to everyone in his life as a boy, and it is not right for a boy to be sexually active. Wade handled his situation by splitting his life—sexual and non-sexual—into two parts.

## Passiveness in the Marriage

Since everyone in the alcoholic home is afraid of open confrontation, passiveness is a strong characteristic in the marriage of ACAs. This comes out in different forms. The familiar one is not taking any action. A person feels unhappy about something the partner does (or does not do) but feels powerless to take action, so she or he sighs, shrugs, and pushes the feelings underground.

Yelling and other forms of acting out anger, such as violence, are actually passive forms of behavior, to the surprise of most people. Why? Because, in the end, nothing is actually done. *I really told her!* you may think. All you did was blast away, impotently; you took no action. You let off steam but only kidded yourself that you acted. You walk away from the incident thinking you have scored a victory, that you have taken a stand, that from now on, things will be different. Wrong. Usually that style of interaction continues—more yelling with no communication taking place, no negotiation done, no contracts made, no follow-through accomplished.

Yelling is an *exploding* style of passiveness—*imploding* is the opposite. That involves turning your anger inward on yourself, perhaps with a force equal to that of the person who yells loudly at the other. This can involve giving yourself guilt messages, criticizing yourself harshly, blaming yourself, taking all the responsibility on yourself. "Well, it's my fault he got angry at me, yelled at me, hit me, got drunk, left me, got involved with another woman. . . ." This person can become a walking compressed tank of anger, that doesn't explode outward—but may implode, collapse within. She may become depressed or have a nervous collapse, or suffer some other damage.

A third type of passive behavior is *overadapting*, obeying the *shoulds* put on you from another person instead of making your own decision and doing what you think needs to be done.

A fourth type of passiveness is *agitating*, trembling, becoming emotionally disturbed.

One component in an unhappy marriage is a low energy level; energy is being drained in negative ways. When a positive interaction takes place, it energizes the partners. When partners are passive: requests are denied; members feel angry at each other; the energy level goes down; the husband and wife feel negative and discouraged about their situation.

## Setting Limits in Marriage

Partners may have difficulty in setting limits with each other. The wife may complain that the husband doesn't help with the children. But after she has attacked him, she feels guilty and withdraws her complaint, more internally than externally. Because she lacks skills to make requests of him and to feel herself worthy of his treating her fairly, she probably will attack, which makes her feel better temporarily. Then she feels she ought not to have said what she did, so she takes it back, either verbally or actively—by continuing to carry all the load as before.

These individuals lack the confidence and the know-how to behave consistently. The wife, in this case, will give total care to the children for a long period of time until some incident will trigger her dissatisfaction. Then, she blasts her husband, he perhaps counteracts and defends himself, and they move off the original subject without resolving anything. Her inner voices of *Don't rock the boat* and *Be all things to all people* cause her to give up her original goal, which was to secure an agreement from her husband to share in the child care.

With Tom and Ellen, when she blew up at him because he "never helped with the children" (which was accurate), he immediately promised whatever she demanded because that was the way he got his hysterical mother to stop screaming, accusing, and making him feel guilty. Ellen, a naive person, subsided, believing his promise. With Mother, though, Tom followed through; with Ellen, he learned that the promise took care of the situation and didn't follow through with specific action.

Part of the problem was that Tom did not know how to help with the children since his own father played a passive role in that home. Tom lacked any skills for dealing with young children, and Ellen did not make specific requests. For example, at one point she demanded that he keep the children each Monday night so she could have a night off with friends. True to form, he agreed (to get her quieted down), but before the next Monday came, through Ellen's own feelings of low self-worth, she had talked herself out of going. "I don't have time and we don't have the money," was her justification to herself. If she had had more effective follow-through skills, probably Tom would have done what she asked. On the other hand, Tom could have helped her by insisting that the carry out her plan. Since both were passive, the situation muddled on.

If someone asked Tom to label himself and his wife according to passive or active, he would call her "extremely active" because of her tirades. Actually, she is as passive as he—unable to take action. This couple lacks effective communication and negotiation skills. They didn't hear their parents make direct statements to the other, such as "I'm feeling angry with you about. . . ." They didn't see negotiation taking place. "Let's sit down and work out something." The children saw either no skills or negative

examples. So, when any situation arises that calls for
expressing feelings directly, making requests, negotiating,
following through, they simply do not know how. They fall
back unconsciously on what they observed in their homes
of origin.

## Trust Problems in Marriage

Low trust can be a problem in these marriages. The
alcoholic is a paranoid personality, and distrusts his family
members, sometimes accusing them openly of lying when
they are not, or he may make his suspiciousness plain in
his words and actions. Edith, an ACA who would never
have dreamed of being unfaithful to her husband, couldn't
understand his jealousy and suspicions. He timed her
when she went on errands and when she came home from
work in the evenings. "Where did you stop? What men
did you talk to?" She truthfully denied his accusations and
learned that this was his father's style. The son assumed
all wives cheated on their husbands (or perhaps that all
husbands accused their wives of cheating). His mother had
not cheated, but the son patterned his behavior after his
father's.

## Competitiveness in Marriage

The ACA couple is *competitive* rather than *cooperative*.
They have difficult attaining a sense of "we-ness." They
lack the skills to communicate and negotiate common
goals; all they know how to do is to push for their own
aims. The individuals are not able to take the long view to
see what this does to themselves as persons, to their
relationship, to the children's development, and to the
family dynamics as a whole. The husband and wife are into
winning. They are unaware that when one wins in this

way, everybody loses and that the individual would win more through working to build family unity and strength.

Each feels the need to guard his territory and power because it is usually true in this type of marriage that it is not safe to release power and space to the partner—he or she will take advantage of it. Even when one partner grows so that she could share power and responsibility, the other person may not be mature enough to operate on an equal level of maturity.

Connie had "agreed" to raise the children singlehanded because (1) Ernest never volunteered to help with the children and (2) whenever she asked him to help, he answered defensively, "I help with the children!" but never came through with practical aid. By the time the children reached the early teen years, Connie had grown in her self-esteem and communication skills so that she started sitting down with Ernest and asking him to share joint responsibility in certain projects with the children. He would gladly agree, but she became angry when he did not follow up. "It's as if I pick up my end of the log and start carrying it, and it feels awfully heavy. Then I look around and see that you're not carrying your end of the log." Connie then refused to share joint leadership with him any more. When a situation came up, she would ask him to handle it or she would do it. For example, when a note came from school regarding one of the children, Connie gave it to him, saying, "I'm not going, are you interested?" and he went.

Maxine married Robert, who then decided to enter the ministry. He became an associate pastor of a church on an unpaid basis since he had no theological training. He entered school and Maxine worked to carry the full financial support of the family. Robert attended each function of their church in the evenings. Whenever his church had a free night, he sought out a revival or some other event to attend in another church. He usually did that on Sunday afternoons, also. Maxine's resentment grew since he gave virtually no help with the children or household chores. She sat down with him and proposed, "If every family member (including the two children) would spend ten minutes picking up just before going to bed, the house would stay reasonably clean and I would not have the whole load on me."

Robert replied affably, "I can handle that." But he did not follow through and the whole load remained on her. Pragmatism demands that partners withhold their trust when they are let down.

On practical and emotional levels, each defends his territory and tries to garner family members on his side. Sometimes the couple competes for the loyalty of the children by trying to paint the other as a villain in the eyes of the children. This has the possibility of backfiring—the attacker can be turned on by the children as they defend the other partner. Even if it doesn't backfire, tremendous emotional damage is done to the children. Thus, the parents actually use the children to fight their battles with their spouses. This is unfair and very hurtful to the children. Usually, they repeat this competitive pattern in their own marriages.

The couple can also compete for the loyalty of outsiders. Dan didn't really want to visit his demanding mother often, so when she pressed him for explanations for infrequent visits, he said, "Well, you'll have to talk to Naomi." Naomi did not want to make the visits, either, but since Dan did not claim responsibility for his own actions, his mother blamed her daughter-in-law for the fact that Dan didn't visit her. His need to have his mother believe he was loyal to her caused him to allow his wife to receive unwarranted criticism and rejection.

In the alcoholic marriage, the sober partner may enjoy her role as the "good" one and would be disturbed if her spouse became sober, became converted, and joined the church, became "good" in those areas which had been her turf. The same dynamic can take place in the ACA marriage: one partner may present himself as "good" in the eyes of the community, often at the expense of the spouse. Wallace was one of the best workers in the church which meant that he rarely gave time to his family. His resentful and overloaded wife withdrew from church activities. The church members, seeing only the surface, criticized her.

## Moving Toward Harmony

If a couple is to move toward harmony in the marriage, they must gain skills in communicating and negotiating. When one makes a request of the other and gets it, she or he feels positive toward the other. In return, the one making the request can stroke the other, promoting a positive air in the marriage and generating energy in the relationship.

*Get to know yourself better to clarify your own needs.* Then you can give clear requests to your partner. Many individuals do not know what they need; out of their own confusion and splitness, they give mixed messages.

Harold accused his wife of not taking enough interest in his work. The next evening, she greeted him with, "How was your conference?"

He turned on her viciously. "You think you have to know every move I make!" She felt confused and angry. Harold has conflicting needs, and he communicates these to his wife. He suffered much maternal deprivation as a child; when his wife shows little interest in him, he needs more attention from her. When she inquires about his life, however, this stirs up his memories of his controlling, paranoid mother who demanded to know every move he made. Harold's wife cannot please him until he first clarifies within himself what he wants from his wife and then makes direct requests of her.

*Second, examine your patterns of relationships to see how you may be repeating your alcoholic parent's behavior.* Barbara and Dick usually slept late Saturday mornings and had a relaxing waffle breakfast. This was the one time during the week they had for sharing and closeness. Each week, after breakfast, when Dick was in a mellow, comfortable mood, Barbara, seemingly unprovoked by anything Dick did at the moment, would go into a tirade, delivering long-term unresolved anger toward him. Dick would think, *What is going on? What did I do to set her off?*

Barbara began to delve into herself and her past to learn why she erupted inappropriately every Saturday. Of course, that was when Dad, drunk, delivered his anger to the family! Dad, a weekend drinker, was sober, quiet, and brooding during the week. On Saturdays, the family learned what had made him angry Monday through Friday.

Without realizing it, Barbara had become programmed to believe that Saturday morning was the only acceptable time for expressing anger. She recalled how she justified repressing it on other days. If she felt annoyed about something Dick did at 10:00 Tuesday night, Barbara would say to herself, "It's too late to get into anything tonight, we have to get up early tomorrow morning," and would hold back from saying anything. It was this stockpile of feelings that erupted on Saturday mornings.

Barbara contracted with herself to become spontaneous about expressing negative feelings even if it were late at night. After all, the Bible verse that says, "Let not the sun go down upon your wrath" (Eph. 5:26) has tremendous practical value. Fresh anger is less hurtful, both to the recipient and the holder than could anger that has festered for a while. Dick, who felt threatened by any show of anger by his wife, didn't like her new style and would try to get her to back off. But she stuck to her guns, being convinced that this behavior was more beneficial to each of them and to their marriage. Because she refused to be intimidated, Dick began to lose some of his fear of anger.

## Countering Burnout

Marriages sometimes get into a state of burnout—the couple is mired down with neither able to make any positive move. If one partner can take just one action to interrupt the downward cycle, which will bring some energy into the situation, there is hope that things can take an upward turn. Lou came to see me, describing a marriage in a state of burnout. After that single appointment, she felt energized and went home and rearranged the den which was such a mess it depressed her and her husband. When he came home and saw what she had accomplished, he felt so good toward her that she reported he treated her in a positive manner for an entire week!

## Downward Spiral Communication

Most ACA couples have a downward spiral style of communication. Here is an example:

Fran and George spent an afternoon at the mall with their baby son. They rushed home to get ready to go to a block party. George stretched out on the couch to rest while Fran fed the baby. The exchanges they had illustrate the downward spiral.

1.  Fran makes a request: "George, will you go up and get the baby's outfit together while I'm feeding him?"

2.  George resists, attempting to get her to back down: "I've got a headache."

3.  Fran feels annoyed. She allows him to make her

defend herself, then attempts to persuade: "I don't have time to do everything. If we're going to be ready on time, I need some help."

4. George continues to resist, adds fuel to his attempt to get her to back down: "I just laid down."

5. Fran gets angrier and justifies her request: "I've worked harder than you and I'm still on duty."

6. George attacks her in an attempt to intimidate her by making a generalized attack, moving away from the specific request: "You expect too much of me."

7. Fran abandons the topic and counter-attacks George, completely off the subject: "You're just like my father. He never did anything to help, either."

8. George, resentful, responds (with justification): "Leave your father out of this!"

At this point, the couple has completely gotten off track and has resorted to personal attacks. This is the standard pattern of downward spiral communication: with each exchange, they move further away from the original focus. Usually the exchange degenerates into personal attacks. Usually four exchanges take place before one party gives in. George "won" because he succeeded in getting his way.

Incidentally, they arrived late at the party.

Those of you who have children, observe how this type of communication takes place when you tell a child to do something he doesn't want to do. Usually four exchanges take place before one party gives in.

How could this have been handled more productively?

The one making the request needs to clarify within herself what she wants and state it clearly. Fran did that. The requester needs to resist the efforts of the other to get her off the track because with each exchange the two get further away from the original request. Fran allowed herself to be drawn into defending her request, while getting angrier. The asker needs to repeat the request at each exchange, without changing one word.

Negotiation can take place midstream. Fran could have asked, "Since you don't feel like helping me, should we decide to go late?" If he agrees, they have successfully completed a transaction which is vital to healthy communication. The focus is on the issue and neither is attempting to coerce the other. In this case, the question would have been, "What time do we agree to arrive at the party?"

Stroke the other party with thank-you's, physical touching, and smiling. Revising communication patterns within a marriage can turn a relationship entirely around.

Recently I saw a new book title: *Good Marriages Take Work*. The subtitle read *Bad Marriages Take More Work*. Probably ACAs must work harder at making their marriages work, to unlearn negative ways of relating, and to master positive ways of interacting.

# 6

# Parenting Styles of
# Adult Children of Alcoholics

As fifteen-year-old Ann came in to dinner, her father walked into his bedroom and closed the door. "Ann's jeans are too tight! They look terrible!" he stormed at his wife, Naomi. "She ought not to wear them." He paced angrily. "She looks cheap." With hands on hips, he glared at his wife.

Naomi glared back with equal intensity. "If you're so upset about it, Dan, say something to her! Don't hop all over me."

"I will," he said huffily, looking at her as if somehow she had not come through with something she should have done.

Dan did not say anything to Ann about the offensive jeans. He did, however, continue to harass his wife whenever his daughter (and the other children) did anything he didn't like.

Dan and Naomi are both ACAs. Neither is alcoholic nor drug addicted, but the atmosphere in the home is similar to that in the alcoholic homes of their childhoods. Both promised themselves as children, "I'm going to do a better job of raising my children than my parents did."

But Dan and Naomi didn't know how. They lacked adequate parenting skills because no one taught them, and effective parenting was not modeled before them.

Naomi said, "My goal was to be the best parent in the world. I read lots of books on the subject before my children came along. But when an actual situation arose, when a child had a tantrum, for example, I reverted to the ways my parents had acted."

## What's Happening in the ACA Home

Here are some of the things taking place in the homes of parents who are ACAs according to Jane Middleton, clinical director, Seattle Mental Health Institute.

*Loop communication.* This takes place when individuals talk about others rather than to them. A triangle is created. A husband and wife might talk to each other about a child's offensive behavior, but no one ever talks to the child. A parent might talk inappropriately to a child about the problems he is having with his wife (and vice versa) rather than to the spouse.

Parents can send messages through a child to their partners. Lauren got a raise in the grocery budget for Mother by appealing to Dad. Dad controlled the money and because he was angry at his wife, automatically he denied her request. Lauren, Dad's favorite, pleaded the case and took the message back to Mom that the amount was increased.

A parent can send anger (and other feelings) through a child to the spouse. For example, a teenager may speak rudely to Mother. Dad might condone that behavior by saying nothing because he does not have the courage to deliver his own anger to his wife. Or Dad might give a verbal rebuke to the child, but his tone of voice indicates that he sides with the child.

A parent may take out on a child her anger toward

her partner. She may lack skills to speak her feelings openly and the repressed emotions come out on those who are the safest objects, the children.

*Difficulty in setting limits*. The parent can be overly strict—set too firm boundaries. The parent might go in the opposite direction and be overly permissive, or inconsistently switch from one to another. Predictability is extremely important in a child's developing trust in his parents.

*Difficulty following through*. Dan and Naomi couldn't tolerate their children's pain, so a child never learned a natural consequence of misbehavior. Either the rule was bent or the child got a tongue-lashing, but no effective discipline was carried out.

In Dan and Naomi's home, many rules were created and quoted but usually Naomi (the involved parent) found a reason to say, "Well, . . . just this once. . . ." Dan's involvement consisted of spouting rules and feeling that he had done his job as a parent by that act. He usually forgot the entire incident and gave no follow-through. The oldest child reacted by becoming very rigid for fear that she might overstep one of the unclear boundaries. Since she didn't know where they were, it was safest to keep still. Ann, the youngest, perceived that the rules existed in name only, so she tested every one and succeeded in virtually knocking them all over. By her behavior, she was begging her parents to set limits, which gives a child security.

*A tendency to parent themselves through their children*. Naomi was so hungry for nurture that she overnurtured her children. If one got hurt, she oversympathized and "laid it on so thick" that the children became self-pitying and had low tolerance for pain. Naomi also presented herself to the children as one who could fix all pain. As the children grew up, the faced great disillusionment when they learned that Mother could not do so. For the oldest daughter, this led to a loss of trust. She learned that Mother seldom kept her promises, so the girl began to rely only on herself. The youngest developed feelings of rage at Mother and at society because Mother had given the children the message that life would be trouble-free. They had difficulties adjusting to teachers because the children expected outside authority figures to be as protective as Mother had been. When special treatment didn't come, the children perceived the teacher's behavior as rejecting, which led to paranoia in the children. When Edie, the middle child, wrote an exceptionally good Halloween story for a third-grade assignment, Mother said, "I know your teacher will say something about this story." At the end of the day, she excitedly asked, "What did the teacher say about the story?" Edie shrugged. The teacher, with thirty-three children, could not single out one child for special attention, no matter how much it might have been deserved. Mother kept setting the children up for disappointment in the outside world.

*Black-and-white thinking on part of all members of the family.* In this home, family members get labels of the "good child," "the bad child" and so forth, rather than everyone being viewed as being real and having shades of gray. Two children could do the same thing, yet the "bad child" gets scolded and the behavior of the "good child" is ignored. Family members do not really know each other very well because they view each other through the preconceived labels. The individuals are usually judged on behavior rather than valued for what they are. They feel reluctant to share feelings with each other for fear of being judged rather than accepted.

*Avoidance of conflict.* Anger is especially threatening to ACAs, so the parents usually swallow their anger or act it out. The children learn these passive/aggressive ways of behaving (acting out anger in acceptable ways when they do not feel free to communicate it directly). A child who pouts or withdraws into silence is acting out his feelings in a passive/aggressive manner. A child who keeps on saying, "Yes, Mother," when told to do a chore but never does it has learned the fine art of passive/aggressive behavior.

*Emotional distancing.* Touching, sharing feelings, and experiencing closeness seldom takes place.

*Parenting by the book* (rather than trusting your own inner guidelines). One mother said, "I raised my children by the rule-of-the-month, according to what I had read that day or week. The children became increasingly confused."

*Consistent guilt about parenting and a belief that there is a perfect parent* (and that you should be one). This places great strain on the parent because she or he can never relax and enjoy the children or the task of parenting itself to the fullest. Their guilt is always saying, "You're not doing it well enough. You must do better." These parents are always spotting new areas of the parenting task to which they feel they must attend. This keeps the family stirred up. No one can ever settle down. The children grow up being compulsive, also, and unable to relax.

*Difficulty with spontaneity and having fun.* These parents are usually workaholics and feel comfortable only when functioning within rigid schedules and rules. They focus on doing rather than being.

*Have little idea of what is normal* (and often set unobtainable goals for family life). Naomi felt that everything she said had to be quotable as if a reporter were following her around to write an article about her mothering style. She said and did what she thought would sound good in print rather than what she really felt.

*Have unresolved grief.* These parents have many issues of loss based on what they didn't get from their alcoholic parents. The ACAs have never grieved sufficiently. That delayed grieving is processed through their own children. The parents overreact to sadness in their children's lives and try to overprotect them from normal sadness and grief in their development.

Claudia Black says that one of the ACA's first tasks is grief work—to get in touch with the sadness lingering from childhood.

*Have a need to be popular with their children.* Out of their fear of rejection, parents can strive to be popular with their children and can feel good when they know the children are pleased with them. This can cause the parents to abandon their roles as parents: they can make decisions based not on what is good for the child but on what will gain them favor with the child. The parents can be obedient children to their children. The parents can be afraid to say no and to set firm limits. The child learns he can use his anger and rejection as weapons against the parent. The children can wind up holding and using power that is inappropriate for them. While this might make them "happy" at the moment because they get their way, it has long-range damaging effects on their security.

## How Can ACAs Develop More Effective Styles of Parenting?

Find out who you are as a person.

Build your own self-esteem.

Allow your child to make choices and live with the consequences.

In an authoritarian home, the parent makes the decisions and tells the children what to do. In that home, a "good child" is defined as one who is obedient. Children who grow up making choices, though, are better prepared for decision making as adults and experience greater emotional satisfaction in their lives.

Parents can start allowing children, even at a young age, to make choices. "Which of these two cereals do you want?" The child must stick with his decision. If he refuses to eat it, then he goes hungry until lunch. The typical parent, though, will feel sorry for the child and will rescue him and give him a third item. When young children have too many items to choose from, they become confused.

Authoritarian parents tend to rescue their children more when they get into a bind than democratic parents who allow the children to make choices. The authoritarian parents are overly involved with their children and feel less detached from their children's pain, so these parents are more vulnerable to rescuing their children. Democratic parents are more detached all along and have less investment in whatever the child decides, so it is easier for them to keep hands off and allow the child to work through his own solution. This helps the child to develop the skills for living, to mature and to feel good about himself.

Authoritarian parents act out of many *shoulds* which means that they make many decisions based upon guilt and "What will other people think?" They evaluate much of their own success as parents upon the perfect performance of their children, so it is harder for them to stand back and allow their children to make mistakes. That might show other people that these parents weren't perfect, heaven forbid! Democratic parents allow their children to be separate individuals and do not feel as threatened if a child makes a mistake.

Here is one formula for effective parenting: *The parent teaches the child, allows the child to make choices, allows the child to reap the natural consequences of his actions (which would include making mistakes), then comes alongside to be a support system when the child makes mistakes and is in pain*. Children then feel less fearful about making mistakes and about revealing them to their parents. They do not anticipate a wrathful response when they mess up, so in these homes, there is less need for secrecy, lying, and coverup. The child feels more willing to take risks and develops more self-confidence.

Our need to control is threatened when we allow children to make their own choices, so when we attempt to shift from top-down to alongside, we may experience much anxiety.

Resist the urge to give your child immediate gratification: When my children were little and whined, "I don't have anything to do," or "I'm bored," I sprang instantly into action, reeling off possibilities. In addition, I would often stop whatever I was doing and help them make homemade play dough or push them in the swing, or whatever. If I had it to do over, I would play the role of dumb cheerleader. I would say, "I wonder what you could do?" When the child came up with an idea, I would squeal, "That's great!" If the idea were unsafe, against the rules, or not feasible, I would have said, "That's a great idea, but . . ." and would have told her why she couldn't do it. I wish I had thrown the burden on their backs which would have stimulated them to become creative and to take responsibility for themselves, and to have delayed gratification until they came up with a solution.

Let me give a word of caution about books and articles giving "How-to's" to parents: the parent may check off everything recommended in a book; the family may go on picnics; they may have daily devotional times; but as long as the family system is dysfunctional, it won't work, and the parent might as well save herself all that effort. The effects of dysfunctionality are so subtle that they can undermine all the efforts of the parents to do "the right things."

Naomi tried so hard to give her children an enriched family life (the kind she didn't have), but several things undermined her efforts. She and Dan had severe marital problems that they were not facing, so each parent had a great deal of unexpressed anger toward the other. When Naomi felt angry toward Dan, she took it out on the children. In addition, her repressed anger toward her husband would come out inappropriately when she was with the children. Most of the time, Naomi was an ideal mother, but occasionally, a child would do a little thing that would cause Mother to lose control and she would scream cutting, hurtful things at the children. They felt greatly confused: "What happened to our good, kind, loving mother?" Those moments of outburst greatly undermined the days spent in doing the approved things with the children.

A second thing happens when the involved parent is unhappily married. She turns to the children for her gratification, so she is excessively active in the lives (and anything that is excessive is unhealthy); she feels off of them to get her badly needed nurture. On the one hand, she is doing enjoyable things with the children, but, underneath, subtle messages are being received by the children that eradicate the "good" things the mother does with them. They are being forced up into the parent position to take care of Mother.

ACAs can become better parents through getting counseling and joining a group with other ACAs where they work through their own loss and grief. Parents Anonymous is a good group where parents can share their frustrations and learn better skills. As they do this, they can become more spontaneous human beings who can be more open and consistent and who can trust themselves more.

Parents can read books on parenting and family. These can teach how families can interact in a healthy manner.

ACA parents can call on trusted friends to pray for healing within themselves and their families.

They can take risks in sharing their feelings with the spouse and children. As they see that this experience doesn't devastate anyone, they can do it more often. They can introduce new words into the family vocabulary and new ways of behaving into the family framework. For example, when Madeleine had been a parent for eighteen years, she introduced the word *hurt* into her family's vocabulary. When her sixteen-year-old daughter flared up at Madeleine at dinner, she said, "That hurt me." About a month later, the daughter told her mother that a certain thing "hurt me."

These parents need to get better acquainted with themselves and give themselves permission to do more things that feed them emotionally, socially, and spiritually. If they take care of being good to the child within themselves, they will then do a more effective job of parenting their own children.

The goals for parenting are: (1) to help the child mature, and (2) to enrich the relationship between the child and the parent. Here are some practical guidelines for more effective parenting.

*Take the focus off the child's behavior and place it on your own.* Keep a checklist on yourself.

Do you give contradictory messages?

Is your behavior consistent and predictable?

Do you place unrealistic expectations on your children?

Do you give your children conditional rather than unconditional love? Do you value them for what they do rather than what they are?

Do you inhibit or forbid free expression of feelings? Do you say, "You shouldn't feel that way," rather than "I see," or "I understand."

Do you indulge rather than love? A loving parent sets limits and sits on his own pain while enduring a child's reaping the consequences of his choices.

Do you create triangles between a child and your spouse or between yourself and two children?

Do you allow for differentness in your children, or do you expect all to fit a certain mold?

Do you make "I feel..." statements and encourage your children to do the same to you?

Do you praise more than you correct?

When you express anger to your children, do you focus on the behavior rather than attack their self-esteem?

Do you develop a rich life for yourself so that your children do not get the feeling that they are responsible for your happiness?

Parenting styles are inherited. If you are an ACA parent, it is especially important that you work to change the parenting behavior you learned so that you will not face the grief of seeing your children repeat those styles when they become parents.

# 7

# Work Styles of
# Adult Children of Alcoholics

"Workplace relationships may echo elements of family relationships unlike others," says Sharon I. Eve, director of recovery services at the Alcoholism Center for Women in Los Angeles. ACAs might expect the home to affect their interpersonal relationships, especially the way they relate to their spouses and children, but it seldom occurs to ACAs that they take the dynamics of their homes of origin into the work setting. Because they are unaware of how their background affects their jobs, they do not see things that can trip them up in achieving career satisfaction and/or success.

Work absorbs most of an adult's waking hours. A job consumes most of a person's physical energy for the day. The career drains the worker's emotional strength. A Christian's work is a vital part of service to God. It is essential, therefore, to give attention and effort to make one's work as productive and as fulfilling as possible. ACAs take feelings and behaviors into the workplace that may block that productivity and fulfillment. Here are some of the ways the dynamics of the alcoholic family show up in the work setting.

# Attitudes Toward Authority Figures

A child depends on the parents for the basic elements needed for survival: food, clothing, shelter, and protection. The way these adults provide those necessities determines how the child feels toward authority figures: trusting, fearful, rebellious. When the ACA gets a job, he finds himself dependent upon the employer in a way similar to the parent: the paycheck provides for the needed food, shelter, and clothing. The adult can then respond to the employer in the way he feels toward authority figures in general.

# Workaholism

ACAs fall prey to workaholism, becoming addicted to work, power, and/or money. The need to succeed controls them rather than vice versa. They may work unbelievably long hours, ignoring their needs to lead a balanced life. This may result in the loss of important personal relationships and can lead to job burnout because of one-track living. Joe, at eighteen, set high goals for himself: by age twenty, he aimed to manage his own pizza house. He reached the level of assistant manager and sometimes worked around the clock, glorying in his stamina and in the fact that he could go long hours without eating or sleeping. A year later, he became engaged. His fiancee broke the engagement because she was tired of dating a young man who fell asleep during the rare movies they attended and who seldom made himself available for any companionship.

ACAs who enter religious vocations can become caught in workaholism on a very subtle level: they believe they are working for God when they work around the clock, seven days a week, twelve months a year, in season, out of season, in health, out of health. On a Saturday morning, a young minister felt warm and a look in the mirror showed a flushed face. A thermometer revealed a fever. "I suppose you're going to contract a supply preacher for tomorrow?" his wife asked.

"Oh, no. I will be in my place," the minister said in righteous tones.

The wife told an older Sunday School teacher the situation on the phone. The woman said, "Tell your husband that good health is good religion." The wife passed on the message, but the husband held to his decision. The result? He missed the entire following week from work, lying in bed, unable to work for God or anybody, and added to his wife's load who had three small children and a heavy schedule at church herself.

The young man viewed God as a hard taskmaster who said, "You must work. Period." The minister projected his parents' voice of "It's never enough" onto God and did not feel free to take care of his basic health needs. Sometimes God calls on His workers to be martyrs, but we need to leave that decision in His hands and not martyr ourselves out of mistaken notions of what God requires.

## Perfectionism

The perfectionistic atmosphere in the alcoholic home can give the child the feeling, "I must be perfect or my parents will not love me," or "What I do is never good enough." The adult worker can experience great anxiety, stress, and dissatisfaction that comes from fairly constantly feeling "not good enough." He can place himself in a dependent position with the supervisor rather than viewing himself as having unique value within the organization that places him on some sort of peer basis. If the messenger boy within a large corporation sees his value to the company, he can see that, in his own way, he is as important as any other worker rather than feel inferior because his salary and status are the lowest of the hundreds of employees.

## Approval Seeking

The ACA can focus his attention on trying to gain the boss's approval rather than using those energies to accomplish the task. A supervisor rebuked a young man for taking a certain action, and he replied, "I did it because I thought it would please you" (which was not true). His voice had a wheedling tone that sounded like, "Daddy, please don't be mad at me." This raised questions about the worker's judgment. Did he make decisions that seemed best for the company or did he take actions he thought would cause "Daddy" to be pleased with him personally?

## Projection

The worker can project onto the boss qualities the parent had: he can perceive the boss as being critical and demanding and can interpret comments as being negative when they are not. The worker could assume that the supervisor would be angry if a report is missing; it would never occur to the ACA that the boss might be tolerant. Recently, I read a woman's account of being sent to fetch the cows as a child. When she reached the woods, she fell into daydreaming, picturing a wounded (handsome, of course) soldier whom she nursed back to health and rescued from the enemy. She reached the barn late, without the cows. Her father smiled. "Sometimes I daydream too," he said. It doesn't take superior wisdom to know that the father was probably not an alcoholic! Since the alcoholic has limited ability to put himself into the shoes of another, he responds to a child's behavior with judgmental responses. ACAs often assume that the boss (the father) has a similarly limited repertoire of behavior.

Since the child became "parentified" in the alcoholic home (children acted like parents to take care of the parents' needs), the adult can relate to his supervisor in the same way. He may think his first task is to accommodate the boss rather than take care of the work assignment or his own needs.

Jackie, a nurse in a convalescent center, became a martyr for the cause of keeping the home functioning. If the boss asked Jackie to work four extra hours a day without pay, she did so. The boss stopped asking other employees to come in on holidays; she knew Jackie would fill in. Jackie denied her own needs as a person and as a mother to relieve her boss of pressure. If she had to work through mealtime, she did so without complaining. If she had to scramble to get a babysitter for her eight-year-old daughter on a moment's notice, she complied. If she got only four hours of sleep some nights—when she worked late and went in early the next day—it never occurred to her to demand consideration for herself.

When Jackie entered one of my support groups, she learned to value herself and her own needs, and she started saying no. In addition, she started taking risks. She talked with her supervisor about how she felt when taken advantage of and taken for granted. The woman replied, "I never knew you felt that way," and treated Jackie with greater respect from then on.

## Caretaking Behavior

Likewise, the adult might find himself drawn, perhaps unconsciously, to dependent employers and the worker finds himself taking care of his bosses in the way he took care of the alcoholic parent and the co-dependent one, and in the way he observed the sober parent taking care of the alcoholic one.

One of my daughters worked briefly as receptionist

for an electrical supply company. After a few weeks, she said, "Mother, I think nearly everyone here is alcoholic. I can see all the traits you talk about in the workers here. For one thing, nobody trusts anybody else." She learned that the owner was, indeed, an active alcoholic. So was the man who interviewed her for the position. The assistant manager behaved like a Co-Dependent, trying to soothe everyone's feelings and trying to placate everyone to keep the "family" functioning. When my daughter received her first paycheck, it was less than agreed upon. She said to the assistant manager, "I want to make an appointment with you to discuss my pay." He avoided eye contact with her while she was talking and avoided her from then on and never gave her the appointment. She handled the situation by finding a different job.

## Dependency

The ACA feels not only the need to be pleasing to the supervisor but also a sense of dependency on fellow workers. Jackie supervised twelve aides, assigning all their tasks. Whenever she wrote names on the board for a specific situation, she felt nervous, fearful that some of the aides would get mad at her or not like her. Always, some clamored, "Don't make me do that. Give that job to one of the others."

Jackie would feel confused, doubt her own judgment, and usually change the assignment. If she didn't, the aides would retaliate by pouting and acting rudely to Jackie. They learned they could manipulate her, so Jackie felt miserable most of the time and confusion existed within the setting.

After being in the support group for several weeks, she had to choose two of the aides to maintain the station while ten went for an in-service training session. She made her choice based on reasoning rather than fear of how they would respond, then wrote the names on the board. One of those chosen to work came up, put her arm around Jackie, and said in a syrupy voice, "Don't make me work, let me go to the workshop."

Jackie answered firmly, "My decision is final and please don't put your arm around me if you're doing it to get me to change my mind." Word began to spread that Jackie was no longer vulnerable to manipulation. She experienced much less anxiety on the job, and the work went much more efficiently than before.

## Fear of Criticism

The ACA has little notion that "I am of value apart from what I do," so in the work setting that can become "I am of value here only as long as I do my work well." Criticism of the work, then, is taken to be criticism of the person himself. A co-worker of mine once threw papers up in the air and stalked out of the room because the rest of us discussed the pros and cons of a suggestion he made. He resigned periodically (to rescind the action after he cooled down) whenever one of us challenged his viewpoint even slightly. It became evident that his self was so strongly tied up with his work that he perceived even a questioning of a proposal to be a rejection of himself. The ACA can spend much time at work nursing wounded feelings and feeling paranoid when the facts do not call for that behavior.

In a similar vein, a man stopped going to church because a motion he made died from lack of support. "I figured they were telling me, 'Ben, we don't want you around any more.'"

## Distrust of Praise

In the alcoholic family, praise was inconsistent or the child might have been manipulated by praise; therefore, the adult might distrust it. If the supervisor praises the worker, he can think, *This can't last. Sooner or later, he will find out how incompetent I really am,* even though the worker may be highly competent.

## Vague Sense of Boundaries

Boundaries in the alcoholic family moved. At times, individuals may not have respected boundaries between persons; at other times, rigid boundaries might have been held. Children did not learn to discern boundaries, so in the work setting, an ACA expects others to take care of him. He might, in subtle or overt ways, take advantage of fellow workers by claiming or attempting to claim time, privilege, or benefits.

While completing my MS degree in counseling, I found a position as a secretary on the university campus. The department secretary exhibited behavior that showed consistent violation of boundaries. She had a private typing service operating alongside (in fact, superimposed on) her job. She spent her day in the word-processing room typing papers for students. One of her assignments was to answer the phone, but a switch on her desk flipped the phone over to another secretary, so the young woman kept the switch on constantly and took care of her subsidiary business.

She controlled the sign-up sheet for the two word processors. When she put up the sheet each Friday afternoon, she signed her name on machine A for every day of the coming week. The rest of us played a catch-as-catch-can game competing for machine B. When she had no typing to do, she "glad-handed" around the department, visiting others, talking in a loud voice. The few hours each week that she did reside at her desk (in a hallway within hearing distance of all the surrounding offices), she talked loudly to friends on the phone, disturbing the work of those nearby. Her behavior said clearly, "Take care of me and indulge me, and I will not hesitate to invade the boundaries of other people in order to get my needs met."

A person who has a vague sense of boundaries has difficulty saying no. He may feel responsible for the work of others in addition to his own. Fellow workers can learn that this person will carry the load for others. Betty resented the fact that her boss dumped the "garbage" work on her each morning. After being in one of my support groups and learning to make "I" statements, Betty said, "Denise, I feel resentful that you give me the 'garbage' work each morning. There are others here who are just as capable as I am, and I think these unpleasant jobs should be assigned fairly."

Denise looked surprised, then called out to another worker, "Oh, Bob. . . ." She never gave Betty any of that type of work again and did not penalize her in any way for speaking up.

A member of one of my groups complained, "I'm so overworked. Everybody else keeps giving me things to do that aren't my responsibility."

"Have you ever heard of saying no?" I asked.

She answered, "Yes, but they don't know the meaning of no." They would if the worker acted on her no rather than passively said it, then complied with the unreasonable demand.

## Rigid Boundaries

ACAs can set up rigid boundaries to "keep their guards up" so they won't be rejected by or absorbed into the family system. The individual who lives bounded on north, south, east, and west by rigid boundaries will keep others at a distance. He may fail to interact sufficiently with others as needed to get the work done, or he may deal with others strictly on a businesslike basis and avoid any intimate contact.

One man walked ramrod straight, greeted others politely but at a distance, talked only when necessary to take care of the work, and had no social contact with fellow workers. The man was due to receive an award in the annual presentation, always held the first Monday of December. When the department head invited the man and his wife to the event, the man replied, "We can't come. We never go out on Monday nights."

Betty, a shy, single woman of thirty-eight, transferred from her hometown of New Orleans to try to establish an identity separate from her mother, widow of an alcoholic. Betty worked efficiently but remained aloof from fellow workers. Extremely lonely, she spent evenings and weekends watching old movies on her VCR. After she came into private counseling with me, I gave her an assignment to invite a co-worker of her choice to lunch the following week. Betty invited a young woman who revealed during lunch that her home town was New Orleans, also. Both liked jazz and pined for the unique po' boy sandwiches from their hometown. At the end of the lunch, the guest confessed, "I thought you were a stick-in-the-mud, but I have really enjoyed eating with you today."

## Control Issues

Since control is the biggest issue for ACAs, this need can express itself when the worker is a supervisor. He may use his authority in negative ways, resulting in low morale and resentment from his work team. Employees may fear him. This supervisor may have a need to always be right and might be the type of person who will say anything to be right, which could include changing policies on a whim to maintain his position. He could exact obedience from his workers rather than treat them as respected workers who have unique contributions to make to the work setting.

This supervisor will stifle creativity and trust within the group, creating the dynamics of the alcoholic home where the employees are treated as inferiors rather than co-workers. They may feel the need to become manipulative to get their needs met. The ACA may be the type who resents any challenge or question from an employee. Misinterpreting it rather than hearing it as an objective question about the design or schedule, the supervisor may take it as a subjective attack and respond accordingly. He may criticize his employees excessively and find it difficult to praise.

Controlling employees are not limited to higher-ups. Sometimes a secretary can have everyone jumping or backing off according to her moods or intimidating behavior.

## Anger on the Job

Since ACAs did not learn constructive ways of delivering anger in their homes, they often deliver anger on the job in passive/aggressive ways (passive on the surface but aggressive underneath). One of the most used is showing up late to work. The worker resents the boss simply because he is the boss, and if any unfairness happens along the way, the ACA lacks the skills to deal directly to correct the problem. Thus, he comes in late more often. His low self-esteem is also at work, so he could have an underlying motive to provoke the boss to fire him, thus confirming his victim position. Nancy had the ability to present herself positively to a prospective employer and she amazed her friends by securing multiple jobs as time went along. Once on the job, though, Nancy started going in late. She would be warned, then fired. She continued on this downward spiral of negative work experiences, unaware of the part she played in the situation. She never stayed on one job long enough to earn status or benefits, so she continually borrowed money from her friends to meet her basic expenses.

## Excessive Loyalty

ACAs developed a sense of overresponsibility in the home, so they sometimes stay in a job that is destructive to them out of a feeling of loyalty to the boss or the company. Maybe the worker is abused by being underpaid, overworked, or treated disrespectfully, but if a friend says, "Then, why don't you find another job?" the ACA responds, "Well, they need me."

## Roles at Work

Work styles parallel the roles the children took in the home. A man called me regarding counseling for himself and his wife and as he told me about their four children, all in their twenties, the careers of the children fit identically the four roles. The oldest child was supersuccessful and had risen to the top in his field before reaching the age of thirty; the two daughters acted out the Mascot and Lost Child roles; and the youngest child, a male, acted out the Scapegoat/Lost Child role.

"He had the opportunity to get a full athletic scholarship to the state university and we are furious with him that he turned it down," the man said. "He just wanders around the country, and when he runs out of money, he comes home. I'm telling my wife we need to get tough with him and stop taking him in, but she can't turn him out." The man concluded, "He has just told us he is homosexual, which we can't understand at all." This is a common pattern in the alcoholic family—one child earns an exceptionally good living and enjoys high status while another will have trouble finding or keeping a job.

The Hero can also take care of people in the work setting. Mary Ellen and her husband owned apartment houses, renting exclusively to low-income workers who paid by the week. Mary Ellen bought supplies for tenants' babies, bought furniture for their apartments, and tolerated late rent or no rent. She especially indulged a nephew and his wife and child. The landlords had a "No pet" rule. The nephew got a cat and argued Mary Ellen into letting him keep it. He delayed paying his rent, since he seldom worked.

A woman tenant not only got a cat, but gave the kittens away to other tenants, thereby encouraging them to flaunt the rule and the authority of the landlords. Mary Ellen read an article in the newspaper in which I was interviewed. With that small amount of information, she learned who she was: an ACA. She revolutionized her work style in a matter of days: issuing eviction notices, (including one to the nephew), introducing written contracts, taking the cat woman to court for nonpayment of rent and for failing to evict. (Mary Ellen learned along the way that the woman was a skilled landlord abuser.) The relationship between Mary Ellen and her husband improved remarkably because he had argued for strictness with relation to the tenants and she had defied him, causing much conflict between them. I've never known someone to grasp the concepts of the ACA situation and go into action so effectively with such a scant amount of information.

The Mascot may focus on gaining acceptance in the work setting by her wits rather than her skills. She often links up with an employer whom she can manipulate into allowing her to play this role in the office. She gets by with things that others don't and uses her charm to get out of tight spots.

The impulsive behavior of the ACA can cause him to make a hasty, unwise decision regarding his career. Joe, the aspiring pizza manager, was transferred to a pizza house that seemed to him to be in a slow-business area. After one day, he quit—throwing away his track record with the company and his dreams. He lacks the ability to assess facts, to tolerate frustration, and to look beyond the end of his nose.

## Tolerating Abuse

Children in an alcoholic home grow up tolerating the intolerable and not even knowing that it is intolerable— they think every home is like that. In the work setting, when abuse takes place, the ACA may not even recognize it. No warning bells go off in his brain, no signals flash. In fact, if he should feel some discomfort and a desire to protest, he may feel guilty for feeling that way. In his home, someone usually gave him the message to stifle his feelings and to go along with whatever was happening. The ACA might work for—and stay with—a boss who functions in that style. If the worker complains, the boss would give the impression that the worker was out of place to speak up.

## ACA Work-Style Survey

Respond to the following questions as they relate to your work environment and workplace relationships.

1. I dread going to work.
2. I attempt to manipulate my supervisor into doing something my way.
3. I avoid direct communication about problem areas, including work environment, work relationships, and work load.
4. I hold my feelings of anger, hurt, fear, resentment, overwork, or being taken advantage of inside.
5. I avoid or ignore problems so as to not make waves.

6. I walk on eggshells when my supervisor is around.

7. I blame myself for my employer's moods and behaviors.

8. I take care of, or protect, my employer.

9. I dread the time when my evaluation comes due.

10. I take responsibility for my assigned tasks *and* those of co-workers or my employer.

11. In general, I have a feeling of overwork and/or burnout (no motivation to perform).

12. I feel as if I can never do a good enough job.

13. I avoid negative feelings related to work by drinking, using chemicals, food, sleep, or other escapes.

14. My good feelings about myself stem, almost totally, from my supervisor's praise.

15. I feel better about myself when I can relieve my supervisor's discomfort.

16. I focus on pleasing my supervisor rather than the task.

17. My actions at work are determined by a fear of rejection.

18. I put my values aside to please my supervisor or co-workers.

19. I respond to criticism at work by feeling inadequate and guilty.

20. I feel overwhelmed by my working responsibilities.

21. I feel guilty about my work some of the time.

22. I experience stress-related physical symptoms in relation to work, such as headaches, "knots" in the stomach, exhaustion, insomnia, agitation, backaches, pain in the neck, or nausea.

23. I accept a lower-paying or lower-status job than my capabilities.

If you answer yes to three or more of the statements, your issues that came from growing up in an alcoholic family may be affecting you in the workplace or the workplace itself may closely resemble an alcoholic family system.

# 8

# Physical and Emotional Health Problems of Adult Children of Alcoholics

In *Co-Dependence: Misunderstood-Mistreated,* Anne Wilson Schaef says that co-dependence is a disease in its own right. "It has an *onset* (a point at which the person's life is just not working, usually as a result of an addiction), a *definable course* (the person continues to deteriorate mentally, physically, psychologically, and spiritually), and untreated, has a predictable outcome (death)." She continues, "We now know that co-dependence results in such physical complications as gastrointestinal problems, ulcers, high blood pressure, and even cancer. Indeed, *the co-dependent will often die sooner than the chemically dependent person.*" People who keep their feelings bottled up tend to have more illnesses, and one of the primary behaviors of ACAs is to repress feelings.

Children of alcoholics have numerous stresses that lead to physical and emotional illnesses. The ways the ACA develops and responds to his personal illnesses often relate to the role he took in the home.

The Hero is usually a superresponsible person when

caring for other people. When taking care of himself, he can be superirresponsible.

Whenever one of my children was sick, I was oversolicitous, sparing no effort (and especially not sparing myself) to make them comfortable and well. With regard to my own health, though, the pain had a hard time getting my attention. I would respond only when it reached an intolerable level. One afternoon, while walking down the street, a sharp pain hit the instep of my left foot. Since I tend to believe that exercise heals all physical complaints (and don't ask me where I got that concept), I walked more than my usual mile that day. For more than three months, I continued to walk with a hurting foot. Whenever the thought came to see a doctor, I shrugged it off with, *I don't have the time*. A fall on that foot, bringing a pain so sharp I could no longer ignore it, took me to the doctor. An X ray revealed a fallen arch. Three years and much expense later, after wearing ugly clodhopper orthopedic shoes, the pain went away. We ACAs are slow to learn that it usually pays to take care of the problem promptly.

While I am typing this chapter, I have a sore jaw that has been hurting for six weeks. First I thought I had stretched my jaw too widely, then it seemed more like an earache. I am still crunching hard foods on the other side of my mouth and still thinking, *It will go away; no need to see a doctor.*

One of my big toes started hurting when the shoe pressed on it. I could live with that. I wore shoes only during the day. Then, the soreness increased, even the pressure of the bedcovers hurt at night. Well, I could sleep on my side. After three weeks, I could not bear it any longer, so I took time out of my compulsively busy schedule to see the doctor. "You have an ingrowing toenail," she said after a quick glance. So there was a reason for the pain! Whenever a physical pain appears, my inner dialogue says things, such as: *Maybe it's because I'm under stress,* which doesn't tally with facts because my health is remarkably good and any illness I have ever had was an overt type, such as the toenail incident. Don't ask me why I attribute the ailment to an emotional cause—that is what hypochondriacs need to do and never do. My second statement is, *Maybe it will go away.* None ever has yet.

After my family arrived in Santo Domingo, Dominican Republic for our third term overseas, one of my eyes started itching. *It's probably a reaction to all the moving and the newness,* I told myself and did nothing (except scratch a lot). The annoying itching continued. When I waked one morning, unable to open my eyes, I went to a doctor. I had pinkeye; think of the people I might have infected along the way because of my delay in seeking medical help!

This is typical behavior responding to that message we received, "It is OK only to take care of others," and to our feelings of low self-esteem. We have denied ourselves as a whole, so we never learned to take care of our physical bodies or our emotional needs. Our behavior is a delayed reaction: even though we may be overly alert in responding to stimuli from other people or situations, our pain message must go through so many barriers that it either isn't heard or is devalued when heard. Rather than responding with quick action, we act sluggishly, when at all.

We do not hear, or we argue with, or we deny signals warning of overload. "I can do this one thing more," "I can rest tomorrow," "I'm really not that tired." We can become candidates for burnout.

These denial and devaluing messages we give ourselves come from the home where we were told (specifically or implicity), "Don't feel what you're feeling" (emotionally more than physically), but we can generalize that message to spread to all types of our personal care. In the alcoholic home, the child's physical health can be ignored or given inadequate care because of the problems in the home: lack of financial resources, lack of both parents getting involved in the child's health needs, lack of the ability of the alcoholic parent to broaden his scope of concern beyond himself, and so forth. If the sober spouse is already overloaded in every possible way, she can respond with indifference to a child's physical complaint. That day, giving a child medical care, which might involve a trip to the doctor without the help of the spouse and without money (in the days before insurance) might be more than the parent could handle.

Pauline, a Hero who had an alcoholic father and was physically abused by the sober mother, fell in her home on a Wednesday night. She did agree with her inner self to go to the doctor the next day (on the way to work), and an X ray showed a cracked pelvis. The woman completed her day's work as a media specialist in an elementary school. She returned to work Friday, but rested over the weekend. By Monday, the pain overwhelmed her to the extent that she did take one sick day.

"How many sick days have you accumulated?" I asked her, since I knew her pattern of reporting for duty even when feeling very bad.

"Fifty," she answered. When I asked why she couldn't give herself permission to take some time off, she said, "The principal is a very difficult person, and I don't want him to get it in for me." That behavior sounds like the fear of authority figures and the need to please people.

When she shared with me that the pain grew more severe as the day wore on, "feeling like an iron hand gripping me," I asked, "Are you taking any painkillers?"

"Sara," she said, with a note of disgust in her voice, "I think people who give in to pain are weak." The underlying message was, "And weak people are to be despised." Being weak was not allowed in our homes, so we hold weakness in contempt and cannot allow ourselves to act that way even when the facts would abundantly justify it. That woman had a cracked bone and couldn't even allow herself to take an aspirin every four hours.

The Lost Child can get lost through depression and/or suicide. He can consider himself unworthy to get medical help (in the same way the other roles do.)

The Mascot can have Attention Deficit Disorder (ADD) with hyperactivity—can be very bright but can't sit still. Too often, he is treated with chemicals, setting him up for possible addiction later on. He can become manic-depressive as an adult.

The Scapegoat can be promiscuous, needing the immediate gratification of sex. Cindy, a grandchild of an alcoholic, pregnant and unmarried, went for her first medical checkup. The doctor told her the pregnancy might be a tubal one, which could endanger her life. She waked in the middle of the night in severe pain in a cold sweat. She lay there, tolerating the pain and thinking, *I'm dying*. She did not have a car and did not call a friend in the apartment who did and ask to be taken to the emergency room. She lay there and took no action, even though she feared that she was in a serious condition.

ACAs can be negligent of their health: They can miss meals or give inadequate time to proper meal preparation; get insufficient sleep, exercise, or recreation; ignore or fail to carry out a physician's instructions or neglect to take medication on schedule. Since they are accustomed to carrying superhuman loads, they may even have an air of grandiosity which says, "I am not vulnerable to the ills like other people are." Feeling different from others can extend even to the health area.

As a group, ACAs experience much anxiety related to low self-esteem, confused identities, and difficulties in forming intimate relationships. This can come out in tension headaches and migraines and can lead to addiction to chemicals for pain.

ACAs can have hypochrondiacal behavior—can have

physical complaints that may or may not be real. They can have ulcers from stress and from hyperactivity of the stomach. Colitis and ileoitis can be found in this group.

Depression, guilt, attempted and completed suicide run high in this population. Eighty percent of teenage suicides come from alcoholic homes. Impulsive behavior leads to self-destructive behavior. Many ACAs are diagnosed as borderline psychotic patients. They are unsure of their feelings and sometimes become psychotic.

They can become pseudosociopathic—they have a conscience, as contrasted with sociopaths, but they are antisocial.

Many become alcoholics or are addicted to other drugs, including nicotine. Oversmoking leads to lung cancer, bronchitis, emphysema, and hypertension. They can take too many drugs, such as tranquilizers or sleeping pills while not becoming addicted.

Eating disorders prevail among this group of people. This can lead to early heart disease, anemia (eating empty calories), and early adult onset of diabetes.

Adult survivors of sexual abuse show many psychological effects of that abuse. They include: depression, poor self-esteem, pseudomaturity or immaturity (fear of age, appropriate dress, manner, or behavior). They can experience disassociation (consistent detachment from emotions and self, frequently feeling like an object).

Somatic complaints of these victims include headaches, lower bowel dysfunction, urinary tract infections, frequently from an early age.

In short, ACAs pay a price for their childhood in terms of their health. Learning to take care of their health needs is an important step toward personal healing for ACAs.

# 9

# The Spiritual Life of
# Adult Children of Alcoholics

Recently I heard a sermon entitled "Why People Reject Jesus." That pastor evidently did not know much about the relationship between abusive fathers and their effects on children because one important reason did not appear on his list: some fathers give such a negative view of God that the children resist any approach to receive Jesus.

A child develops his view of God based upon the image he has of his earthly parents, primarily the father. Cecil G. Osborne says in *Prayer and You*, "There are exceptions, but in general, it can be said that at a *feeling* level, God is like one's human father."

William De Arteaga, specialist in inner healing of memories says,

When a person is injured by the father, his ability to relate to God is impaired. If his primal image of the father is one that is hurtful, his ability to view God in a healthy way is fractured. No matter how much he wants to read the Bible and follow God, if his image of the Abba Father, which Jesus describes, is a drunk person, the child has a severe impediment to prayer, growth, and holiness.

"It was hard for me to say the Lord's Prayer, the first prayer I learned as a child," says Judy, a forty-one-year-old nurse. "I'd skip over 'Our Father' and start with 'who art in heaven.'" Both of Judy's parents were often drunk when she was growing up in Miami, Florida.

Judy's father either made sexual advances toward or he "slamdunked" the children. "He beat Mother also. We knew all the emergency numbers to call, all the places to hide." When Daddy deserted the family, Mother seemed to collapse within. She just couldn't cope. Her drinking accelerated, and Judy blamed Daddy for that. "I had a lot of hate toward my father."

Ellen's father, a deacon, taught the Scriptures each Sunday in his Baptist church. During the week, this alcoholic father physically and sexually abused his daughter. Ellen became alcoholic herself, married a physically abusive man, and became obese through food abuse. She entered Alcoholics Anonymous to conquer her drinking problem, divorced her husband, and joined Overeaters Anonymous. There, she came to believe in God. "It's no thanks to you Baptists that I came to a position of belief!" she said to me, admitting that she had some negative feelings toward me when she learned that I am a Baptist. Understandably, it is difficult for her to be free of negative feelings toward that denomination. The mother in the home, who tolerated the abuse of the child, was also an active Baptist, compounding Ellen's feelings of abandonment and therefore, resentment.

Sam's father criticized every move the children made as they grew up. The father seemed to be unable to praise and was "always right." Since so much was going on in the home that was negative and painful, and since Daddy never acknowledged that anything was his fault, Sam concluded it must have all been his fault.

Rachel's father would buy a beautiful dress, show it to friends and boast, "Look what I bought Rachel." After he got the desired praise from others, he returned the dress to the store. On occasions such as a birthday party, Rachel, who was diabetic, would beg to have a soft drink. Daddy would say, "I'll give you one. Come into the bedroom with me." There, he would pour some of the soft drink into a paper cup, go into the bathroom, and come out and hand the foul smelling mixture to her and say, "Drink it."

The two would return to the party where guests would observe Rachel not drinking the soft drink. When they would urge her, and she would say, "I don't want it," she came across as a petulant child who begged for something and then wouldn't drink it.

Daddy's cruelty extended into more specific areas than the soft drink episode. He also abused her sexually. She is unable to have children due to internal damage.

Joyce serves in a Christian vocation and is married to a minister of education. This woman exemplifies Christian graces and behavior—she has helped to create a home where her mother, divorced from her alcoholic husband, lives. Joyce's brother, Robert, however, will not listen to any "God talk"; he verbally and physically abuses his son. Two wives have divorced him. The difference in the behaviors and personalities of the two ACAs probably lies in the fact that the father treated Joyce kindly, but physically and verbally abused Robert.

Tess's father does not abuse his children in any overt way, he simply drinks himself to sleep on the sofa after dinner every night. "The deepest thing we can ever discuss at the table is the weather," Tess reports. Daddy doesn't abuse, but Daddy doesn't *father* his children, either. He is abusive by what he *doesn't* do.

**Some Ways an Alcoholic Parent Impacts on
the Image the ACA Has of God.**

*The ACA may develop a fear of God.* Osborne says,
"The fear of God can be the beginning of neurosis—or at
least a warped personality." Some ACAs believe themselves to be agnostics or atheists when the reality is that
they don't *know* God—they view God as being like the
father who instilled fear in the children. Osborne comments that "an hour's dissertation on the love of God can
not wipe out the feelings of a lifetime." Osborne sometimes counsels such troubled individuals to pray to Jesus,
since the term "God the Father" has highly negative
connotations for adults abused as children by a father.

*The ACA may view God as being absent.* Osborne
continues, "An absentee father can mean an absentee
God." This absenteeism can take place actually or emotionally. One man said to me, "I don't know why my wife
gets so upset about my two drinks before dinner each
evening—I've been district sales manager for my company
for twenty-eight years and have earned a very high salary."
The children had only a nodding acquaintance with their
father, and his alcoholic personality exaggerated the situation. Even when at home, he did not take any real interest
in them.

Sometimes the alcoholic parent drinks quietly in the
home and can be present bodily but emotionally absent.
The children may not know that Mother is alcoholic
because she may go to her bedroom and drink by herself
at the end of the day. Although physically present, her
alcoholic personality prevents her from relating closely to
the children. They feel emotionally abandoned.

A thirty-nine-year-old daughter of a quiet, home-
alcoholic mother disagreed with me when I described that
type of person as unable to relate closely to family members. "My mother and I meet often for lunch and have a
wonderful time sharing." When I asked what they talk

about, the daughter replied, "My sister's problems." So, the "wonderful sharing" turned out to be a familiar triangle—two people talking about the absent third person, a perfect example of the point I made.

When the parent is absent physically, the child can justify the lack of companionship because there is a reason that can be seen. The child can also kid himself and think that the parent would spend time with him "if only Dad didn't have to travel in his work." However, when the parent is in the same room or in the same house, yet isn't there emotionally, the feelings of abandonment are very strong.

Children who experience emotional abandonment (which is inevitably present in the alcoholic home) can view God as distant, indifferent, unloving, powerless to act on the person's behalf, and cold. These adults may have no background for taking their problems to God. They may assume that God is unapproachable and that they are unworthy of God's showing interest in them or of God's using His power on their behalf.

Martha Lee is married to Bert, an ACA who isolates himself in the bedroom and is emotionally absent. Her first husband was an ACA, also. Her twelve-year-old son, Earl, lives with her. Earl frequently asks his mother, "Will you pray to God for such-and-such for me?" Martha had not made the connection between Earl's relationship to his two fathers and this behavior. "He knows that I have a close relationship with God, but evidently he feels that God is inaccessible to him."

*God may be viewed as weak.* Mary's alcoholic father stayed in bed a lot. "His God representation for me was weak, helpless, lily-livered." Based on this type of father, ACAs sometimes see God as powerless, even a Being to be despised or pitied. These children do not develop any concept of God as a Being filled with majesty, omnipotence, strength, a creator who sustains the world and cares for His people.

*God may be viewed as judgmental*. A hostile, punitive father, Osborne points out, can leave a child with a feeling that God is angry and judgmental. Osborne had experienced feelings of fear toward his father, so he felt that God was stern, demanding, and ready to vent his wrath upon all who had sinned. The alcoholic personality is a judgmental personality, and the child is judged, often on an unfair and unrealistic basis. Behavior that was approved, maybe even applauded, one day might bring punishment another day, according to the sobriety of the parent or a change in mood. In projecting the father onto God, the child finds experiencing Him as a God of grace, forgiveness, and support difficult.

This feeling of being judged often causes ACAs to feel that God is displeased with them. If asked to specifically name their sins of the moment, they might give vague answers. All they know is, "We feel that God is displeased." They feel they must do more to earn God's good favor. It is hard for them to believe that God accepts them just as they are, so they try to gain status with Him by performing good works. They essentially have a religion of works not of grace.

Bert and Martha Lee have many discussions about "grace" that always turn into arguments. Bert seems to feel that he is earning God's approval only when he is working within the church setting. He takes part in weekend lay missions nearly every weekend of the year. Twice a year, he makes trips to the foreign mission field with lay teams.

Martha, dedicated to the Lord, is unhappy within the marriage relationship because Bert is rarely at home for the couple to have any companionship. She believes that she is being a Christian in her work setting and within the family as well as when participating in church activities—

in short, being a Christian all of the time rather than only in specific settings. Whenever the couple talks about grace, Martha says, "That means that God accepts us just as we are, that we don't have to work to earn His favor."

Bert answers, "Yes, but. . . ." His life-style indicates that he works around the clock trying to gain acceptance from God. Bert did not gain acceptance from his alcoholic father, and it seems as if Bert has projected this characteristic onto the Heavenly Father.

*God may be viewed as demanding perfection.* Close to the judgmental aspect of the home is the perfectionistic atmosphere: Nothing the child does is right. The alcoholic parent is impulsive and impatient. A slow, inadequate, or incorrect response from the child brings rebuke and punishment rather than an offer to instruct the child how to do the task right. Adult children develop into perfectionistic individuals and view God as expecting perfectionism. They usually become rigid persons who overdo everything they touch. If they perform a task halfway or in any way defectively, they are extremely displeased with themselves. They can be among the best workers in the church but can experience little joy in those tasks or in the relationship with the Lord.

Jeanne says that the perfectionistic atmosphere in her home made her develop a legalistic view of God and religion. *If I'm good, God will love me,* she thought. She realized she could never be the perfect person the Bible describes, so, *If I can't measure up, why should I try?* she shrugged. That led to her staying away from God for ten years. Now she experiences God as giving unconditional love—love not based upon our performance but based upon God's nature.

*A controlling father represents a controlling God.* Control is one of the biggest issues for alcoholics, and the child grows up in an atmosphere where he feels little freedom in his actions. He has difficulty understanding a concept such as free will. Believing that he has options with God is hard. He may feel like a puppet being pulled by divine strings.

*The ACA can have difficulty feeling forgiven by God.* Forgiveness is often absent in the alcoholic home. This type of conversation rarely takes place between an alcoholic parent and a child who has blundered: "I understand how you feel because I have felt the same way," or "I can understand how things went wrong because I've had a similar experience." An alcoholic has limited ability to put himself in another's shoes since his viewpoint is self-centered. The message the child receives, either directly or subtly, is, "Be perfect or I condemn and reject you, and you are a terrible person for doing (or failing to do) what you did."

The child finds it difficult to believe that God forgives when he fails, and he has difficulty forgiving himself. His "self-talk" is full of *shoulds* and rebukes. "You blew it again!" or "I should have done that differently" accompanied by feelings of self-disgust. Hitting yourself with *shoulds* is a waste of emotional energy and thought time since the past can never be recaptured. A person can evaluate his behavior and learn from past mistakes, which is a different process from rebuking oneself about the past.

The person who feels judgmental toward himself also relates that way toward other people. Judgmental Christians often have status in their churches simply because they usually carry a hefty share of the work load, therefore, they are viewed as "good Christians." Yet they experience or express little love as a part of their total makeup. They often have little success as soul-winners because non-Christians do not feel drawn toward these Christians nor to the God they represent. Fellow Christians do not enjoy these individuals.

Many years ago, a husband and wife in the church where my husband was pastor tried to keep all the rest of us in line with their rebukes. All of us felt strain when in the presence of this couple. One night, when the husband uttered one of his typical rigid statements, I thought, *I don't believe even the Lord enjoys Mr. and Mrs.____!*

*Developing trust in God may be difficult.* Developing the ability to trust, in general, is one of the most important tasks that needs to take place in the child before the age of five—and that rarely happens in the alcoholic home. The child is then severely limited in his ability to trust anyone or anything. Broken promises, emotional distancing, and outright abuse bring about a lack of trust in the parents.

Since trust is the basic element in any faith relationship, an ACA experiences strong barriers to trusting God. The task for the ACA is to develop a healthy view of God. It is possible for a person to be in a relationship with God but to hold an unhealthy and inaccurate view of Him. The child may become a Christian, may even (in fact, often does) become a religious worker, but may hold a view of God that is not biblical or satisfying to the person.

"Since I couldn't trust my father, what made me think God would come through, either?" Jeanne asks. She finds it hard to "relax and trust God to take care of me when there are things I can't control." Jeanne sees that the issues in her faith struggle go back to issues with her parents. "When the Bible speaks of 'seeing through a glass darkly,' I realize that I saw reality through certain lenses when I was a child. Now I need to see things differently. I resisted growing up, and I viewed the world as hostile and uncaring. I felt I ought to fix everything and felt guilty if I didn't."

An Episcopal priest whose father is alcoholic says, "Predictability is one of the most important ingredients in a trust relationship." Because of the unpredictability in her home, Jeanne had difficulty believing in God's unchangeability. She discovered that the only way to overcome this lack of trust in God is to take risks. "When I do that, my anxieties go sky-high," she admits. "I have to constantly re-let go. When I see I don't get 'zapped,' then I can relax and trust more." When she turns loose familiar feelings and situations, "my whole earth shakes. But, I'm aware of the anxiety I'm feeling, and I know that God is not like my alcoholic father, and I'm making progress in viewing God as He really is and in trusting Him with my life."

*Christian ACAs often experience little joy in their spiritual lives* because of their perfectionistic concepts of God and of His expectations. This also comes from the home where feelings were repressed. These adults have little acquaintance with spontaneity as a whole. ACAs also feel a need to always be in control, and allowing oneself to experience any light feeling is threatening. ACAs view religion and God as very serious—the thought of relaxing and enjoying God and one's religion seldom occurs to ACAs.

*ACAs develop excessive feelings of guilt.* The alcoholic home is blame- and shame-based. The alcoholic usually finds someone else to blame for his drinking, so the child grows up in a home where blame is tossed around like a hot potato. When it comes to one member of the family, it is quickly thrown to another. "Shame on you for drinking!" "Shame on you for making me drink!" "Shame on you if you talk outside the home about the problem." "Shame on me for being such a bad child that my daddy is bad." These are some of the hidden and overt shame statements that take place in the alcoholic home. A child does not have the ability to process such statements realistically, therefore, he absorbs the responsibility for what is wrong in the home.

*It is hard for Christian ACAs to accept their negative sides.* Wendy Frederickson, alcoholism counselor in Atlanta, says, "They deny feelings of depression, anger, sadness, tc. They feel that they should constantly rejoice because have the Lord in my life.'"

When I studied in the hospital chaplaincy program, tudents had the assignment to visit patients and report on 1e visits to the supervisor. One day, I visited a buoyant oman who had had a sudden mastectomy. While on acation, she discovered a lump in her breast and the octor rushed her to the hospital. This whirlwind experi- nce left possibilities for emotional responses of a wide amut, but she acted so cheerfully that I joked, "I'm going ) visit some patients who need a chaplain."

My supervisor told me to visit the woman again, ointing out to her that depression often sets in later with mastectomy patient. He felt it would be especially true 1 her case because of the speed of the events. When I ntered the room another day, her husband, a stone-faced 1an, stood beside the bed. "When you get home," I egan to the wife, "away from all the people and activities .ere, you may find yourself feeling some depression. How lo you think you might handle that?"

Her husband cut me short. "Christians should never eel depressed," he said in a Moses-on-the-mountaintop one of voice. I said no more. Later I wondered about the voman. If depression came, what did she do? Surely she vouldn't have shared it with her husband—he would have ondemned her. Probably she wouldn't have shared it with er pastor either. She might have assumed he felt the ame as her husband and would have judged her also. If he humans close to her gave her the message, "Repress ny negative feelings," could she have shared them with ;od?

*ACAs may find it hard to develop a closeness with ;od* because members of an alcoholic family have prob- ems with emotional intimacy. How can we draw close to ;od whom we have not seen when we cannot relate losely to human beings whom we have seen? Many ACAs

would say they have a close relationship with God. Y
Bert Lee, for example, comes home from work or a chur
function, eats dinner, and retreats to his bedroom. F
does extensive Bible study and has lengthy times of praye
But when he comes out of the bedroom, the only ways l
is able to relate to his wife and stepchild are to give the
verbal abuse or to withdraw and act as if he doesn't kno
they are alive. Emotional intimacy is so threatening to hi
that he must isolate himself from the family. It is imposs
ble, then, for him to experience emotional intimacy wi
God.

## Ways ACAs Can Develop Trust in God

Osborne points out that various factors may modify
intensify the impact the father has on the child, such as
strong, warm, accepting mother lessening the influence
a rejecting, punishing father. Some other loving ma
figure—uncle, grandfather, or neighbor—may help a chi
gain a more realistic, therefore, more loving image of Go

When Judy's father left and Mother collapsed, sl
gave the children away. They first went to a coun
children's home in Macon, Georgia. They went to tl
local Baptist church with all the other children. "This w
the first time I went to any formal type of church, b
whenever Mother had gotten into real trouble, she ha
run to the Catholic Church and lighted candles. Rarely-
things had to be pretty tight—Mother paid respects ar
prayed. I would sit and look at a statue of Mary—
peaceful-looking woman in contrast to my usually drunke
mother." On the Seminole Indian reservation, where Judy
family usually spent summers with her mother's family,
old Indian "Granny" (no blood relation), who also did a b
of "mumbo jumbo," took the children to the nearl
Catholic mission. "That was the only time we bathed
Judy chuckles. "We'd wash off in the creek."

In the Baptist church, Judy felt confused. She didr

ee the familiar candles or statues. Her clown nature came
ut. "Where is the water you wash your hands with?
Vhere's Joseph? Where's Mary?" she piped up loudly.
When are you going to say the 'Hail Mary'?" A smiling
udy recalls that the Baptists looked at her "real funny"
nd laughed.

Sunday School teachers taught Judy about God and
bout how He wants us to live. Nature also spoke to this
ensitive child. "I didn't know what all of it was about, but
knew there was something," Judy reminisces. "When I
vatched storms and saw the intensity of the lightning and
hunder, I knew that no man was out there pulling switches.
Or, when I saw a flower, something stirred within me."
udy probed holes and turned over rocks and felt amazed
t the life she saw. "I tried to swim like a fish and nearly
lrowned myself. I learned which kind of snake you could
grab and which kind to stay away from." In the midst of,
nd in spite of, her traumatic childhood, God communi-
ated to the child. "I began to believe that God is an
inseen Being who is very powerful."

After bouncing from orphanage to orphanage, Judy, a
unaway and a troublemaker, was sent to a girls' reformato-
y at age sixteen. A woman who worked with juvenile
lelinquents took Judy to church. The pastor asked a
:hildless couple in their fifties, "Would you mind taking
his girl to be a companion?"

The husband died shortly after that, and the widow
ook the girl into her home. The woman gave Judy some-
hing she had never had before—unconditional love. Judy
egan to wonder about the deity her "mother" believed in
nd talked about it. "She taught me that God is like her. I
vatched her help the poor through the church, going each
lay to serve food. She also helped prisoners, shut-ins, the
lderly. I wanted to be like that."

Judy's conscience began to grow. "Things I had done,
uch as stealing, weren't fun any more. I now knew they

weren't right. When teachers explained the Ten Commandments, I listened. Things the Sunday School teachers taught me in Macon fit in with my new learnings."

Judy became a nurse so she could help people like her "mother," and found work in an alcoholic and drug unit in a hospital. Through her work, she learned about alcoholism and recognized that her parents were alcoholics. She started attending Alcoholics Anonymous meetings to learn more about her parents. She then joined Al-Anon, the organization for people who have a drinking member in their families, and started on the twelve-step program based upon the AA steps.

"The first step, *We admitted we were powerless over alcohol, that our lives had become unmanageable,* let me know I didn't cause my parents' drinking. I always felt I did. The second step let me know there's somebody there who's able to help me." That reads: *Came to believe that a Power greater than ourselves could restore us to sanity.* When Judy heard, "Let go and let God," she thought, *No indeed! He's botched it up too many times. Let Him get outta town! I can do it better.* She viewed God as uncaring, unloving, even cruel. "If you are God, how come you let all this happen to me?" she hurled at Him many times. At Al-Anon and AA, Judy listened to other people's stories. Most of the alcoholics were children of alcoholics too. "I started getting in touch with what God was all about. My anger subsided."

The third step, *Made a decision to turn our will and our lives over to the care of God as we understood Him,* led Judy to respond, "I think I'm going to let Him help me." She says, "I'm happy with my spirituality now. I relate to God, Christ, and the Holy Spirit as if they were real people. I talk to them daily."

*It may be hard for ACAs to hear God's voice.* Within their minds, the *shoulds* sound so strongly that they can override the voice of God. First, since it was OK only to take care of others in the alcoholic home and not to value oneself, the ACA can make all choices—from vocation to marital partner—based on that *should*.

When Dan graduated from seminary as a minister, he felt God's "call" to pastor a church near the home of his parents. Today, he acknowledges that the real "call" came from within himself. His mother had impressed upon him so strongly that he had to stay near her and take care of her that he mistook his mother's voice for God's. He actually never consulted God about "Where should I serve?" He now muses, "I wonder what place God actually had in mind for me?"

The second reason is this: our need for control is so strong that it is hard for us to release any of our own ideas or ambitions long enough for God's voice to get through to us. We may be faithful in having daily prayer times, but we may actually be talking to ourselves rather than listening to God.

When ACAs break through the barriers to faith, they are capable of experiencing a close, warm, and meaningful relationship to God. They can use their pain to become compassionate, caring Christians to help other people who have experienced pain in their lives, as well.

# 10

# Forgiving the Alcoholic Parent (and the Sober One)

Jeanne, at age thirty-five, drove three hundred miles to have a specific conversation with her parents. After two divorces, she felt she had to talk with her mother and father. Her first husband wanted to stay in the marriage but made it plain he wanted to have relations with other women. Jeanne, unable to accept that condition, left; the second husband divorced her. Jeanne, now a Christian counselor in a Southern state began to see a connection between her family background and her destructive relationships with men.

"I prayed half the way down, and plunged in before I lost my nerve," she said. She asked her parents to sit with her at their breakfast bar. "Daddy," she began, "please help me because I've had difficulties in relating to men. I hope God can use this talk with you to heal me." Asking for help caused her parents to relax, but when she said, "Daddy, I see that you have chosen to be a practicing alcoholic," he bristled.

"You don't have any right to tell me what to do in my own home."

"You are right," Jeanne admitted. "I forgive you for

146

the hurt and anger that causes inside of me. So, when you drink, I won't pretend those feelings aren't there, but I want to take them to God. I love you. What you're doing hurts me, but I accept you as you are. You have the right to live your life the way you want to." She paused. "Will you forgive me for judging you and trying to change you and not giving you unconditional love?"

Jeanne then turned toward her mother. "I forgive you for allowing what happened to happen. Will you forgive me for judging you and for being angry toward you because it was safe to give you the anger I felt toward Dad? I'm not going to continue to hold onto resentments. I'm going to honor you no matter what you do with your life."

Alcoholics can seldom hear another person because they are so very defensive, so when Jeanne said, "Daddy, I felt that you gave me attention as I grew up to make Mother jealous," his answer surprised her.

"That was the last thing I had in mind, but I understand that's the way you felt." Jeanne knew that God was very present because her father actually *heard* her.

"Mother, I felt you have been jealous of the attention Daddy gave me, therefore, I couldn't trust your love to be unconditional. Forgive me for getting into drugs and doing things to worry you."

Jeanne concluded by asking her parents to pray with her. The three of them held hands. Mother and Jeanne wept softly and Daddy revealed by a soft facial expression that he felt touched. "Help me with any negative feelings and ways of relating—just negative connections—I may have toward my parents. Break us free from the destructive binding we have had and bind us together in God's love. Help me to honor them. In Jesus' name, Amen."

The two women went to wash their faces, and Daddy walked out to the yard. Each parent appeared to feel uncomfortable even though the atmosphere was very tender.

Jeanne recognizes that acting out the ideals of that

prayer will be a "forever" process, especially when the behavior does not change. And these behaviors have strong power over family members because they have been going on for generations. But this woman *chose* to forgive, an act of the will, and God then worked on her emotions.

When Jeanne's parents visited her recently, she shared with her father, "I believe the Lord is leading me to start a non-profit counseling service." She felt the need to give up the role of the child who must achieve in the family. She also felt afraid Daddy might not love her if she stopped achieving according to worldly standards, especially since she doesn't know if he is a Christian. Jeanne had a secure position in the family—always gaining acceptance—but "I worked myself to death to keep that position. I felt afraid that if I ever stopped achieving, the acceptance would go."

In response to that statement, Daddy asked, astonished, "Where did you get an idea like that?"

Jeanne explained, "Over the years, I felt that sometimes you did not show attention to the other children. When I wondered why, I assumed it was because of the achievement."

He assured her, "I love you and don't worry about things like that." This exchange set her free from some of the negative binding that had taken place over the years and helps her continue to forgive her father.

## Why We Have Trouble Forgiving Our Parents

One of the primary reasons we need to forgive others is because we feel angry about the way they have treated us. The need to forgive the alcoholic parent seems obvious since most people recognize that the behavior of the alcoholic leaves family members angry. In the book, *Of*

*Course, You're Angry,* Rossellini and Worden say: "We're not going to find an angrier person in the world than an alcoholic, unless, of course, we look at the spouse and kids of an alcoholic. . . . We have special problems with anger."

ACAs can be fully aware that they have not forgiven their alcoholic parents, and they can even feel resentful that this burden is thrust upon them. "I didn't do anything, and now I feel guilty because I'm committing a sin by not forgiving him."

William De Arteaga of Atlanta explains: "Under the Western concept of sin, it is something you *do*. I steal, I lie, I lust, for example. The other half of the biblical definition of sin is that we are born into a fallen world and sin *happens to us*. The person is born into a family where sin was predominant, and although the child didn't sin, he may respond in a sinful manner. One example would be that the father abused the child and he hated his father."

The terms *active sin* and *reactive sin* might be used to describe what De Arteaga is talking about. The child who is born into an alcoholic home and is abused may respond with *reactive sin*. That type of sin we need to confess, and we need to forgive the one who sinned against us. We also need to forgive the parent for the emotional abandonment experienced, as well as overt abuse.

De Arteaga also says that we need to receive forgiveness for judging our parents since judgment comes back upon us.

Rossellini and Worden echo De Arteaga's principles when they say, "It is not only the alcoholic who needs to enter recovery—the family members need to recover, as well. Learning to deal with our anger and resentments, learning to forgive people who have hurt us, and learning to forgive ourselves for the wrongs we have committed can be the most important elements in our own recovery."

Many children of alcoholics are not in touch with their anger, but most are aware of their anger toward the alcoholic parent. It sometimes baffles people (both within the family and without) when we speak of the need to forgive the sober parent. Some ACAs come into counseling, puzzled, asking, "Why am I so angry at my mother when Daddy was the alcoholic?" Surprisingly, research shows that often the child feels more anger toward the sober parent than the alcoholic one. There are several reasons for this.

*It is safer, and easier, to deliver anger toward the sober parent.* The child has a more secure relationship with this parent. The child perceives that acceptance from the alcoholic parent is so fragile that the child, out of a need for self-protection, does not rock the boat. The anger the child feels about the home situation must come out somewhere (or be repressed), and when the child feels that the sober parent gives him a strong enough love that he can risk sharing some anger, he does so. The sober parent is often aware of this anger and can feel baffled and resentful. *I'm the parent who's on duty in this family, so why does ____ act angry and sullen toward me and not toward her father?* she wonders and often counterreacts with punishment.

When the child feels enough security with the sober parent to express some anger openly, this produces a healthier situation for the child. The sober parent is usually unable to allow this expression because of the stress she is under and because she doesn't understand what is taking place within the child. It is actually a statement of confidence when the child expresses anger toward that parent.

*The child observes that the sober parent allows herself to be abused—emotionally, verbally, perhaps physically—and does not take action.* The child's sense of fairness causes him to protest this behavior. He feels powerless to do anything himself so he looks toward the victimized parent to defend herself and to set some limits on the abuser's behavior. When this doesn't happen, the child feels angry.

When we place expectations upon a person and those expectations are not met, disappointment and anger follow. The child learns to stop counting on the alcoholic parent for anything of substance—either in the relationship or in overt action. The child then turns toward the sober parent as the responsible one who is viewed as capable of action. When that parent fails to take effective action, the child feels let down and becomes angry.

A director of a battered wives center said: "We get exasperated with victims who don't get themselves out of the situation but we must put ourselves into their situations and their value systems. Look at the options these women have." The director told of a woman, the wife of a medical doctor, who lives in an affluent section of a large city. Twice a year, when the man gets drunk, he batters his wife. Her options are to leave quietly or to leave with fanfare (identifying her husband to the public as a wife-beater), which would humiliate him and ruin his practice and hurt her financially. If she should leave, she also faces the humiliation that comes with admitting that she married that kind of person. The woman's self-esteem is a strong component of the entire picture: she feels that she deserves to be abused. Her lack of support is a factor also: her mother will not support her leaving. Thus far, the woman has stayed.

*The child may be angry because she reports abuse but the sober parent does nothing to protect the child.* The abuse may be physical and/or sexual, and the mother may deny that it is happening. She may, however, acknowledge the report as factual but not take action. The child may not report the abuse and may be angry because the sober parent does not perceive what is taking place. It is believed that, in most instances, the mother knows about the sexual abuse but turns her head, virtually participating in the abuse. This makes the child a double victim—of the hurtful parent and the powerless one—providing grounds for rage within the child.

*The child may feel angry because the sober parent stays unavailable emotionally.* This parent may show kind behavior to the child, but because she feels devastated by living with alcoholism, she is unable to come out from behind her glass wall emotionally. This leaves the child frustrated, hurt, puzzled, and feeling abandoned. ACAs have many unmet needs since neither parent was available emotionally.

*The child may resent the fact that the mother gave him the alcoholic father.*

*The alcoholic parent may be the more "desirable" parent to the child.* For example, Doris, thirty-eight, says, "I identified with my alcoholic father because my mother was so passive—I couldn't identify with that. Also, I resented the mothering I had to give my mother. She confided in me, going beyond what is appropriate for mother-daughter confidences. Finally I had to protect her physically. At thirteen, the oldest of four children, I attacked my father when he hit her—yet again—and me. I blacked out, but 'tore into him' so violently that a younger brother had to call a neighbor, a hefty probation officer, to pull me off. Later, my mother made me apologize to my father. He continued to threaten to hit my mother and the younger children, but he didn't until I went to college five years later, when he resumed the beatings. So I actually became the protector of the wife and children, a function a child shouldn't have thrust upon her. I felt my mother should have taken action to prevent that happening to me." Although Doris feels furious toward her father, she feels equally furious, in a different way, toward her mother.

Estelle recalls, "My alcoholic father was handsome, charming. I felt proud to be with him in public." She remembers her mother as "sour, disagreeable." A child does not have the ability to process why the sober parent behaves as she does—the child only responds emotionally to what she sees through immature eyes.

*The child may be angry because of the load thrust upon her.* Anna, now thirty-five, grieves the loss of her teenage years. From age eleven on, she had to come home from school and prepare dinner and supervise the younger children. Her life became anxiety-filled when she couldn't measure up to the demands, especially when the younger children wouldn't obey her and Anna was then held responsible for any problems that arose. When her mother came home from her job (which she held because the father didn't work), she gave Anna no praise for the monumental tasks she accomplished but criticized her because the dishes weren't washed. Anna felt the greater anger toward her mother.

Anna has only one child. "I cannot bear to have any more because mothering stirs up all those feelings I had during those years when I was the real mother in the home."

This situation illustrates the irony of this home. The parent who puts her shoulder to the wheel to take care of the family is exhausted and burned out and becomes the "bad" parent to the children, the one who scolds and behaves toward them in almost totally negative ways because of her stress level. The anger the children feel is legitimate, but the sober parent is unfairly labeled as the one deserving to receive anger.

*The powerless position of the child brings a response of anger.* When we feel abused by another person, if we feel we have the power to bring about a change, we feel less anger than we do when we feel helpless to change the abuse. The child feels powerless, hopeless, maybe even despairing, which can bring a response of strong anger, even rage. The cornered animal is most likely to attack.

Feeling boxed in with no place to turn can produce strong feelings of fear and anger in a person.

*The child feels anger because he is required to repress other feelings.* Anger is what is called a *second-order emotion*. That means that another feeling, a *first-order emotion*, triggers the anger. Some examples of first-order emotions are: hurt, sadness, loneliness, anxiety, shame, discouragement, devastation, disappointment, fear, guilt, isolation, rejection, uncertainty, abandonment. The person may feel stupid, trapped, unloved, worried, betrayed, misunderstood, left out, ignored, or devalued.

A person who is in touch with his emotions can recognized and respond to the first-order emotion spontaneously and can deal with them appropriately. That would include talking to the offender and requesting some change for future interaction. This avoids the buildup of negative emotions and inappropriate handling of them.

People who have learned to repress their emotions feel the first-order emotion on a very subtle level because the *Child* in us (where emotions are felt) flips the emotion over to the *Critical Parent* to handle. The *Critical Parent* takes that first-order emotion and moves it quickly to the second-order emotion: anger, criticism, judgmental feelings, hostility, resentment, or defensive attitudes. The terms *Child* and *Critical Parent* come from Transactional Analysis. *Critical Parent* has no relation to our actual parent—that term refers, instead, to all the "oughts" and "shoulds" we developed within our minds as we grew up, whether those messages were actually given to us or not. A person who is required to repress his feelings "stockpiles" them, so he can have an unbelievable amount of stored anger.

*The child can feel angry because he is forbidden to feel anger.* The child is living in a situation that can range from frustrating to dangerous, which can bring a wide range of emotional responses from the child, many of them negative. In that setting, the message he receives from the sober parent is, "Don't feel angry about this." Other relatives and the community might also give this message to the child, leaving the child feeling totally unsupported.

Jo says, "My sober mother treated us very kindly and rarely rebuked us. The few scoldings came when any of us showed any emotion of any kind. If we children started a normal quarrel, she would immediately appear agitated and hush us up. The strongest rebuke I ever got from her was, "Wipe that pout off your face." We were living in a horrible home situation and not only were we supposed to behave perfectly but we were also supposed to *look* happy! That made me feel even angrier. It would have felt so good if some adult could have said, 'I understand that things are awful, it's OK to feel sad.'" Jo continues, "I recognize now that my mother viewed my facial expressions as defiance and that threatened her sense of control, but my 'pouts' were more expressions of feeling sad and unhappy."

*The child views the sober parent as "healthy" and fails to understand that living with alcoholism makes her as sick as he is.* The ACA often feels impatient about the sober parent's behavior. "My father died years ago and my sixty-two-year-old mother is now married to a wonderful man; why does she still behave the way she did when she was living with an alcoholic husband?" Peggy, thirty-nine, asks.

"I feel so annoyed with my mother," Ron says. "My father is now dead, and Mother is free to do anything she wants to. But she does nothing but sit around all day, sighing and talking about how tired she is. I know that as long as my father was alive, Mother felt trapped and did not feel free to pursue her own interests. She's now free to get on with her own life, and she isn't doing it!" he ends, disgusted.

# How Can We Move Toward Forgiving Our Parents?

A young woman, Gretta, called me, saying, "I don't have the money to see a counselor on a long-term basis. If I come to you for one appointment, can you help me forgive my parents?" Since counselors need to be cautious about promising specific results to a client, I answered, "Since individuals vary so greatly, it is difficult to predict what could happen in one session." She persisted, apparently in real pain, "But do you have a formula you could give me in just one hour that I could take away and work on?" Again, I hesitated to promise anything specific. "Forgiveness is a process, so it is impossible for me to give anyone a one-two-three step to achieving that."

Gretta joined one of my support groups and began to share her stress with others. A few weeks later, when another member raised the question about forgiving the parents, she commented, "I think forgiveness is a process." She began to make slow, but definite, progress in that direction.

One problem Gretta faced dealt with the question, "If I forgive my parents, must I be in a relationship with them?" A single mother with three young children—two of them hyperactive—she became so upset whenever she saw her parents that she came to the conclusion that the only way she could keep her own life in order was to cut off all contact with her parents. Gretta, a strong Christian, deeply desired to settle the issue of forgiving her parents, but the thought of having ongoing contact with them felt so threatening that that became a barrier to forgiveness.

Forgiving the parents and having a relationship with them are two different issues. If the ACA can separate those, possibly he can move toward forgiveness. After he is able to forgive his parents, he may then view them in a new light. It might not be easy to relate to them, but the ACA may be able to handle the entire situation differently.

As Rossellini and Worden say: "There's no 'quick fix' for any problem with human emotions." Without locking the process of forgiveness into a mechanical formula, we can give some guidelines for moving in that direction.

*ACAs need to understand that just because the alcoholic partner may no longer be present, the sober one is still caught in the maladaptive behaviors she developed while living in the alcoholic situation.* We could use the analogy of a frog jumping out of a pond onto land. Taking the frog out of the wet setting and putting him into a dry one does not change the nature or behavior of the frog. Without professional help and group support, the sober parent usually remains caught in the pattern of co-dependency.

*The ACA needs to erase his expectations of the sober parent.* Peggy, for example, keeps needing a relationship with her mother that she, at present, is unable to give. If Peggy can accept her mother's limitations, she can stop setting herself up for continued disappointment and frustration.

*We need to put ourselves in the shoes of the sober parent.* This can help ease negative feelings. The child may have resented the fact that the sober parent did not divorce the alcoholic partner or take other actions. If we can completely identify with the feelings of the sober one and with the circumstances, we may come out convinced that we would have behaved identically. That can help remove our feelings of, "She should have done thus-and-so."

*The ACA needs to work at seeing the parent as a person primarily rather than as a parent.* As long as we view our parents in that role, we may continue to feel impatient with them. If we can detach ourselves to the extent that we can see Mother or Daddy as individuals with their own struggles and needs, we can relate to them free from the constraints of the earlier relationship in which we expected them to meet our needs just because they functioned in the role of parents. We can shift to being friends with our parents. We can then enjoy them more and let go of some of the old resentments that grew out of unmet expectations.

*We can forgive the parent as a powerful aid in bringing about our own maturity.* In that act, we step from being the dependent, demanding child to the caring, concerned adult. We say, whether openly or privately to God, "I accept that person with all his flaws. I give him unconditional love." If unconditional love has never been experienced in your family, you can be the one to introduce that concept. It might even be emulated!

*The ACA can pray for the healing and growth of the sober parent, as well as for the alcoholic one.* The prayer needs to be offered without strings attached. If we place expectations for certain desired outcomes, we again set ourselves up for disappointment and frustration. We cannot control the behavior of the parent, but praying for her or him can help melt the bitterness within our hearts.

*We can look at our forgiving skills as a whole.* Those skills are not learned in the alcoholic home, as a rule. We possibly have a severe deficit in that area in our total Christian life. Occasionally, an adult explains to the child, "Your father is sick," or "He doesn't mean to act the way he does," so the child grows up less free from resentment than the one who hears directly or indirectly that the drinker is mean or sinful to do what he does.

*We can first forgive ourselves.* How good are you at forgiving yourself? A person unskilled in forgiving doesn't forgive anybody—especially oneself. When we forgive, we are the most like God we will ever be, and that includes forgiving oneself.

*We can recognize how unforgiveness affects our relationship to God.* Jeanne saw that unforgiveness affects her ability to trust God. She now feels motivated to forgive the individuals who have hurt her so she can move any blockage in the flow to and from God.

*We need to forgive to break the cycle of alcoholism in the family.* William De Arteaga says, "It is the lack of forgiving the parent that dooms the child to marry a spouse like the alcoholic parent. It is this dynamic that perpetuates the sick family system rather than the fact that the parent is alcoholic. If we wish to have healthy lives for ourselves and our children, we must break the cycle by forgiving our parents."

*We can make a decision of the will to forgive, rather than wait for our emotions to feel like forgiving.* We then turn the emotions over to God to work on them. We will probably find the feelings returning over and over, but we can affirm the decision to forgive—a conscious contract with God to forgive. Anita carried her load of unforgiveness of her alcoholic father for more than fifty years. One day, as she sat having her daily devotions, she thought, *Daddy is dead and gone. Why do I need to carry this load of unforgiveness around? It's not hurting him and it's hurting me terribly.* She made the statement to God, "I forgive my father." No lightning flashed, no thunderbolts crashed, but she felt a peace because she had made a conscious choice to forgive. In the coming days, she repeated the statement to secure it with God and within her mind and emotions. After years of feeling that she could never forgive her father, the actual event turned out to be quite easy.

*We can model forgiving for our children.* Specialists in this field say that ACAs take on the identical behaviors of the alcoholic with the exception of taking up the drinking. That means that our children may be placed in the position of having to forgive us when they become adult grandchildren. Perhaps we can show them how by forgiving our parents.

*Desiring to obey the scriptural injunction to forgive can aid the ACA*. Lewis didn't start forgiving his father for his drinking until his mother died. Neither Mother nor Daddy had the ability to plan ahead for the future, so for some time Lewis had paid the monthly payments on the home where his parents lived. After the funeral, Daddy asked pathetically, it seemed to Lewis, "Are you going to let me live here?" That had been Lewis's intention, and he continued to go there and cut the grass weekly as he had for a long time.

"As I pushed the mower, I'd see Daddy sitting on the front porch. He looked so lonely. I think he felt very bad physically—he was a diabetic and the doctor had forbidden Daddy to drink. I think he had a lot of guilt and remorse and had little reason to live." Lewis, for the first time, saw his father's pain. "All the years of his drinking, I saw only my mother's and our (the children's) pain."

One day, Lewis was reading the Bible verse where Jesus said that if we don't forgive others, God can't forgive us. "I wanted to clean my life of any unforgiveness, so I asked, 'Who is it I have not forgiven?' My father's name immediately came to mind. I confessed that to God and he forgave me. I then felt compassion for my father and gained some awareness of his pain. He had developed no relationship with any of his children, so when Mother died, Daddy had no one in his life at all. I was able to see him then as a lonely old man rather than just be the resentful son I had been before."

Lewis began to learn that alcoholics are exceptionally sensitive people and that sensitivity—the vulnerability to being hurt—is part of the motivation for drinking in the first place. He recalled that his father's family always spoke of Daddy as being the tenderhearted one. Lewis became interested in knowing his father's broader personality—not just the alcoholic one—and learned much about his father and his background before Daddy died.

For Lewis, the desire to be a compassionate person and to have his Christian faith operate in every facet of his life led him to be able to forgive his father.

June learned that we attract people like ourselves, and she wanted to attract forgiving types of people. One day she hugged her father and although unable to say the words out loud, she thought, *Dad, I forgive you. I know you didn't mean to hurt me the way you have.* Her attitudes toward him changed, and when she sent him the annual Christmas card signed with her usual, "Love, June," she received one in return from him, signed for the first time in her life, "Love, Dad." Who knows what got through to him by way of some mysterious process?

June used the *empty chair* technique to forgive her grandfather who had sexually abused her. She sat across from the chair, pretended he was sitting there, and spoke directly to him. "I forgive you for what you did to me. It was very wrong, but I love you, anyway."

*Confronting the parents may clear the way to forgiveness.* Will, at forty, found himself in a counselor's office at his wife's request. Problems in the marriage had escalated until she called for some definite change. The couples' counseling proceeded well. His wife learned about ACAs and told Will, "I believe this background has a strong effect on your total personality and on our relationship." He discovered more about the topic and saw the connection between the past and his present feelings toward his parents. After much agonizing, he felt convinced that he needed to gain release from all the bottled-up emotions of a forty-year accumulation and saw that that could be accomplished only by talking with his parents. His alcoholic father has been in recovery for several years and is now a deacon in a Baptist church. Although relations between Will and his parents were cordial, Will didn't want them in his home and he rarely contacted them on a spontaneous basis.

Will "tested the waters" with his parents one Saturday by saying to his father, "I'm not going to make the same mistakes with my children that my parents made with me." Dad's eyebrows went up, inquiring. Nothing more was said that day, but the next Saturday, Will drove the long distance to his parents' home, crying most of the way. He knew he had to do this, but he had no way to predict how it would come out.

Will opened the conversation by telling his parents he wanted to talk to them about something important to him. He told of the hurt, the frustration, and the anger he felt during his growing-up years. He used strong terms, at one point saying, "I hated you."

His parents listened. Then they talked. Mother said, "I just had no idea that our problems affected you children this much."

Will continued to pour out his pain, recalling how Dad had been fired from his job because of theft of a large sum of money. Again, his parents talked, clarifying that Will, as a child, had misunderstood what actually happened. Dad had "borrowed" from the petty cash fund each week at work to buy liquor; the following payday, he replaced the "loan." When the petty cash fund turned up short twice, Dad was let go. The parents explained some other situations about which Will, out of his immature perceptions and limited information, had gained incorrect impressions. Will felt better when he learned the facts. (This often happens in a confrontation—the ACA has mystery areas in his life cleared up that came about because of confusions and withheld information. This usually leads to better feelings on the part of the ACA.)

The parents and their son continued to talk and to listen to each other. The meeting ended with Will embracing his parents, crying, and telling them how much he loved them. He cried all the way home, but the tears came from a different source. He and his parents now have a great deal of contact—visiting each other, talking on the phone, and touching. "That is what's so great," Will says. "Before, we never touched."

His mother said, "I'm so glad you talked to us; what if you hadn't?" Will has seen a spillover effect in his marriage now that he has resolved hostilities with his parents. He is a more loving and open human being in every area of his life.

Cheryl grew up in a home with two alcoholic parents. When she was eleven, her mother left and Cheryl took on the responsibilities of the mother. Relatives told Cheryl that her parents were sick, that it wasn't their fault they acted the way they did, so she can't recall ever feeling angry. In a support group, though, she began to get in touch with those buried feelings. When Dad came to visit her that Thanksgiving, she said, "I just want to tell you how awful it was for me while I was growing up."

Dad began to be defensive, saying, "But I stopped drinking and I stayed."

His daughter said, "Dad, I'm not blaming you, I'm just telling you how I felt." Her seventy-year-old father then told her, for the first time, that his father was alcoholic and had physically abused him. She saw that he was as much a victim as she was. Cheryl and her father felt much closer, and forgiveness was easy for her after she had a broader understanding of why he behaved the way he did.

*Gaining understanding of alcoholism can aid in forgiving.* Ralph, now a counselor, learned through his studies that the alcoholic does not want to be caught in the habit of drinking any more than the family wants him to be. "I felt so grateful that I didn't have the pain and struggle that my father did by being addicted to a physical substance. I was able to stop blaming him by seeing that he did not willfully choose to act that way. I gained some understanding of his pain and I released all my negative feelings toward him."

Evelyn said, "I recognized that a person had to be in a lot of emotional pain to need to keep himself anesthesized with alcohol."

*Forgiveness can come through inner healing of memories.* Inner healing of memories is an approach by which a counselor trained in that field leads the client to invite Jesus into his memories to heal them. William De Arteaga states that there is evidence that the developing fetus perceives the emotions of the mother and father. In the alcoholic home, in many cases, the child is not wanted in a direct way, or may not be wanted for what he is. The father may say, "This baby's got to be a boy," and the child is a girl. The counselor can lead the adult to go back into the womb and into memories after birth to heal the memories of rejection.

Carolyn De Arteaga (Mrs. William) describes the process she follows, which she calls "Trinity Healing." She first prays to God, the Father, to give wisdom and discernment. She then asks the Holy Spirit to lift up for healing a particular memory in the person. She then asks the client to invite Jesus to come into the memory as a friend. The counselor then asks the client to report what is happening.

When Mrs. De Arteaga takes people back to reexperience birth, individuals often sees Jesus as the doctor. They consistently report Jesus as "having such kind eyes." One woman who had been told repeatedly by her alcoholic mother that she was unwanted experienced Jesus holding her as she was born. She felt comfortable, loved, and wanted.

A fourteen-year-old girl had a stepfather who beat her mercilessly when he was drunk. The memory that came to the girl's mind was when she was six and brought home a new reading book from school. The stepfather told her to read it aloud, but she had not yet learned how. When she couldn't, he started beating her with a stick. First, the girl saw Jesus coming out of the closet. "Oh," she said, "that's the closet my stepfather used to lock me in when he didn't want to be bothered with me." Closets had been a source of fear for her all her life, but she then felt safe toward them.

Jesus went over to the stepfather, took the stick away, and the man started crying. Jesus held the girl a minute. "Oh, no," she said, "He's putting me into my stepfather's arms. I don't want that." Then, she relaxed, "It's OK. Jesus is putting His arms around both of us."

Mrs. De Arteaga has noticed this pattern: Jesus first deals with the abusive parent, then the hurting child, and then reconciles them. The counselor says next: "Will you tell Jesus that you forgive your stepfather because unforgiveness hurts you, not him?"

Mrs. De Arteaga dealt with an attractive woman in her forties who had a severely neurotic and alcoholic mother. As a little girl of five, the woman had to take care of the household tasks because her mother spent days in bed weeping. The memory that came to the client's mind was a day when she had to do the laundry on the wringer-type washing machine. She couldn't reach it, which was frustrating because she couldn't complete the job. She also had to miss playing with her friends. The child felt very sad. Jesus came in, healed her memory, and the woman reconciled with her mother. The daughter has gained some insight into how damaged the mother was as a child. Although the mother continues to be an inadequate parent, the daughter's feelings have changed so she is able to have a relationship with her mother.

This couple points out that the person's habits of thinking negative thoughts and feelings toward the abusive parent may continue for some time after the actual forgiveness takes place. The individual may feel discouraged, setting perfectionistic standards for himself, expecting instantaneous cessation of the hostile feelings. Mr. De Arteaga compares it to ringing a bell in a tower. "After you turn the rope loose, the bell rings a few more times because of the momentum. People may continue in the old habits, but if they have forgiven their parents, they need to reaffirm to themselves and to the Lord what has taken place within their spirit to break the momentum that has been underway for many years."

In one woman's memory, she took Jesus home with her. The mother ran around, distressed, saying, "How could you bring Him home like this? Everything's such a mess."

Jesus walked over to the mother and said, "Unless you forgive *your* mother, you cannot love your daughter."

She said testily, "I can't forgive that old biddy for all the things she did to me." Jesus then prayed to the Father for this mother, and she forgave her mother. The client was then able to forgive *her* mother.

Mr. De Arteaga emphasizes that this approach is a ministry, not a technique. "We can work until we are blue in the face, but if the person is not willing to forgive, then nothing happens."

In conclusion, we can remember the words of Jesus on the cross, "Father, forgive them; for they know not what they do" (Luke 23:34). No alcoholic parent ever intended to be hurtful. We can also remember the spirit of the words of the Lord's Prayer, "Forgive us as we forgive those who do things against us." As we look down the line into future generations, into the lives of our children, our grandchildren, and beyond, we want to do all we can to break the cycle of alcoholism and its consequences in the lives of our family members.

# 11

# Dealing with a Drinking Parent (and the Sober One)

## Dealing with the Drinking Parent(s)

In *Guide to Recovery*, Gravitz and Bowden say: "A common reaction (of ACAs) is wanting to save your parents from alcoholism. This can be a way to avoid dealing with your own problems." They continue: "You do not need to deal directly with your parents or their drinking. You do not need to educate them, fix them, or confront them. You have more than enough to do just dealing with yourself." They add that while ACAs will want to acknowledge the feelings they have within themselves regarding their parents, the question of whether to confront them is a separate issue. The parent(s) may be dead but it is still important to work through your feelings toward them. This would best be done with professional help.

At this point, let me say a word about seeking professional help. It is unfortunate that in our society seeking counseling for help with emotional or relationship problems carries a stigma. This seems to give Christians a problem: they seem to feel that if they have faith and if

167

they pray their problems will work out. This mentality does not carry across the board in all situations. If a Christian has a cavity in a tooth, he does not trust the Lord to heal it. Without giving the matter any deep thought, he makes an appointment with the dentist. The same would apply to a broken bone. But when it comes to problems resulting from damaged emotions, Christians give themselves *should* messages and feel guilty if their trust and prayers do not resolve matters. I would like to support any reader in seeking counseling, guilt free. Dealing with an alcoholic family situation would be one situation in which a person should not expect to deal with the problem alone.

Children are not going to cure their parents. The children did not cause it and they cannot cure it. Gravitz and Bowden emphasize, "The best thing you can do for your parents now is to take care of your own recovery."

## Focus on Yourself

In the alcoholic family, members focus on the drinker: they learn to react to his behaviors and mood changes; they take responsibility for the drinking; they sometimes try to control the drinking; they try to get him to change. Forrest, in *How to Live with a Problem Drinker and Survive*, says, "Everyone who is living with a problem drinker is believed to become emotionally disturbed as a result of the alcoholic's effect on the family's life-style."

ACAs, therefore, need to shift the focus from the problem drinker to themselves and acknowledge the reality, "I am sick." This would be on a continuum. Some ACAs are healthier than others. When the ACA says, "I am not responsible for the drinking of my parent, I am responsible only for my own health," he has begun recovery. The same term that is used for alcoholics and addicts is used for the children and spouses: they need to enter recovery because they are sick. What constitutes recovery for an ACA?

Join a support system. Al-Anon is excellent for anyone who is in a close relationship with a drinker. This group promotes *detachment* with love. This term needs explanation because many individuals hear this as indifference, withholding help, being callous and uncaring. Detachment means to stop trying to control the other person. It means recognizing the other person as an autonomous, responsible individual (even though he or she is not behaving that way now). It means to stop feeling guilty for the drinking. It means breaking the enabling process that has been taking place. (In many instances, the detachment of the Enabler promotes the beginning of recovery on the part of the drinker.) It means making a choice about how the ACA spends his emotional energies and actual efforts: he will work on himself and his own personal growth rather than try to change someone else. It means getting in touch with one's powerlessness. Family members often believe they truly have the power to control the drinking of another person. This is far from true, but family members delude themselves.

The only person who can stop addictive behavior is the addict himself. As long as family members are telling themselves, and each other, that they can control the drinker's behavior, he or she will believe that, too, and will continue to heap guilt onto others and will refuse to take responsibility for his or her behavior. This is all a part of the enabling process.

## Develop a New Communication Style

Forrest says that typically the sober spouse begins to talk down to the alcoholic. This behavior can spread to the children. The ACA can monitor his behavior, asking to what extent he talks down to the alcoholic parent. Even though that parent may behave like a three-year-old, the ACA can make a conscious effort to talk person-to-person to this parent. That will communicate a hidden message that "I expect you to act like an adult." Talking down to someone gives him permission to act like a child.

As mentioned in the material that dealt with dysfunctional communication styles, members of this family get into the habit of saying the same things over and over to each other. Deborah's mother is a gourmet cook. When she invites her children and grandchildren to dinner, she sets a delicious meal on the table. Everyone sits down and Mother says (as she has said at every dinner for twenty years), "You all go ahead and eat. I'm tired from cooking. I'll just have a drink first."

As the dinner progresses, each family member says (as each has said at every dinner for twenty years), "Mom, aren't you going to eat? The food is great. . . . Come on and eat." Mothers eats nothing and drinks until she passes out, usually about 2:00 A.M.

In a group session, when Deborah presented the dilemma of what to do, I asked, "When are you going to stop saying the same thing? It accomplishes nothing and all of you are participating in the enabling process. You are trying to control your mother's drinking and you don't have that power."

"What I'd like to tell my mother is that I'm not going to come back any more because I don't want my small children to grow up seeing their grandmother getting inebriated at every dinner we eat there," Deborah said. That would be saying and doing something different. As long as the family members participate in the drama, it enables Mother to keep on playing the same role.

Dad's birthday was coming up, and Polly expended a lot of thinking time and emotional energy on the prospective phone call she would make. On all calls in the past, she had spoken to him about his need to enter treatment for his drinking and the two would wind up yelling angrily at each other. The day arrived and Polly read her Al-Anon book to get direction. By 8:00 that night, she had decided that it was not her place to try to get her father to change. She turned the problem over to God and placed the call. The two had a pleasant conversation with Polly giving her father best wishes for his birthday and with Dad inquiring about her and his little grandson. Polly felt pleased with the day she handled that episode.

When Kristen's mother calls from another state, drunk, Kristen says pleasantly but firmly, "Call back sometime when you're not drinking."

### Remove Yourself Physically

As mentioned in an earlier chapter, a young mother of hyperactive six-year-old twins has concluded that for right now, she cannot even see her parents. She gets so upset that she cannot handle her responsibilities adequately.

Muriel is divorced and has a hyperactive nine-year-old son. Because of the many DUIs her father has received, he is not actively drinking but is almost as difficult to deal with as when he was. She attempted getting her son and his grandfather together for what she fantasized as being healthy interactions. She spent the day at her parents' home, and the game plan called for the two males to rake leaves together. Before long, Muriel had to bring her son in and call a halt to the activity because all she heard from outdoors was Dad's constantly berating the child with "You're not holding the rake right! You're doing it wrong!"

The boy became so frustrated that Muriel had to spend time with him telling him, "It's not your fault. You didn't do anything wrong. Grandaddy has problems."

When her son was three, Muriel took him to her parents to baby-sit while she took a night class, but her mother said, "Your daddy feels so jealous of the boy that I just can't keep him any more." Her mother had wound up with two three-year-olds on her hands.

If the alcoholic parent is physically abusive, the ACA should feel completely free to stay away. The same goes for verbal and emotional abuse. In our society, we have been slow to recognize that the damage done in those two areas is just as hurtful as the physical violence. We tend to think that until the physical occurs, children ought to maintain relations with the parents. If the ACA is receiving verbal and emotional abuse, he or she will pass it onto his or her children (not to mention the hurt done to the ACA). He or she must do everything possible to prevent this abusive style of interacting from passing on to future generations.

In a large ACA meeting, a twenty-eight-year-old woman posed her problem: "I have just moved here from several states away. Both of my parents are alcoholics and I think the only solution for me is to move far away and get a job and get on with my life. My teenage brother and sister are begging me to come back to help them deal with the situation. Am I being selfish in pulling out?"

A woman in her mid-fifties said, "My older sister agreed to stay at home with our alcoholic parents when she was about your age, and she is still there. I support your leaving rather than staying and trying to rescue your parents and your brother and sister."

That might strike many persons as harsh and uncaring. But *as long as someone will agree to stay to take care of a sick person (of any category—hypochondriac, depressed) this can be a motivation for the sick person(s) to stay sick.* This lies at the heart of the enabling process. The sick person (or someone else, such as siblings, relatives, or friends) succeeds in making someone feel guilty and responsible for solving the problem. That person gives up his own life and sacrifices himself to rescuing the sick one.

The cycle gets going—the more the rescuer works at rescuing, the more the sick one needs to be rescued. It is possible that all will go under. If the nonalcoholic gives himself permission to pull out, it is possible that at least one person can have a satisfactory life. There is no way to predict how this will go. The parents may never achieve sobriety, and the child can hit himself with guilt for not staying (and friends and relatives may do the same thing to the child), but there is greater hope for some health in the total situation when the child feels free to extricate himself from the mire.

## Do an Intervention

An intervention is the process whereby the family members (sometimes joined by work associates) confront the alcoholic about how his behavior impacts them. This must be done with the aid and supervision of a person trained in this approach. The therapist coaches each person to write a simple, direct message about certain behaviors the alcoholic did while drinking and the feelings the other person had in response to that behavior. The speaker remains objective and refrains from getting emotional. The therapist works with the group until each has worked out his statement and believes he can deliver it nonemotionally.

The alcoholic is invited to join the group for the intervention. The family has packed the alcoholic's bags and transportation is ready to take the drinker to a treatment facility. Each person speaks, beginning with the decreasing order of influence on the drinker. The spouse, for example, often has the least influence because the drinker has learned to tune her out. The final speaker is the one with the greatest influence on the drinker, possibly a child. Each person makes statements essentially including these parts: This is a certain behavior you did while drinking; I felt thus-and-so about it; I feel confident you would not behave that way unless drinking; I care about you; please enter treatment.

Some therapists report 100 percent success. If the drinker agrees but attempts to postpone entering treatment, the family members use all their persuasion to insist that he go immediately. Usually if the person delays, the effect is lost and he does not enter treatment.

One famous example of this approach was when Betty Ford's family used the intervention technique to persuade her to enter treatment for alcoholism. Anyone who is interested in exploring this possibility needs to contact an alcoholism therapist, agency, or hospital chemical dependence unit.

## Dealing with the Sober Parent

For many reasons, the ACA sometimes has a better relationship with the alcoholic parent, especially if she or he has entered recovery. The ACA often has greater difficulties dealing with the sober parent. Each ACA must work out his or her own way of dealing with the parent.

Ada, forty, happily married with two teenagers, gets calls from her father from another state, attempting to draw his daughter into a triangle with the alcoholic mother who spent time in treatment. "Your mother's drinking again," he complains. At first, Ada allowed herself to be drawn into the action and got angry and gave advice (none of which Dad followed). Ada had gone through the family program with her parents. She then joined a support group, so she began practicing the skills of detachment. Now, when Dad calls and delivers the complaint, Ada says, "Dad, tell me about your golf game." Dad loves to play and loves to talk about his games, so he is off and running. Soon, though, he remembers the purpose of the call and returns to the subject of Mom. "What happened on the ninth hole?" Ada gets Dad back onto the golf game.

She successfully maneuvers the conversation until the two hang up. During the conversation, she steps outside of herself and observes how she is handling the situation. She congratulates herself on not getting drawn into what is going on at home, on not allowing herself to get angry, on not allowing herself to get caught in giving advice. By the time she gets off the line, she is smiling. She has not allowed the call to ruin her day and upset her relationships with her own family or the tasks she has to do.

Mom calls Polly at 11:00 P.M. to talk about her problems with her alcoholic husband. "I'm sorry, Mom," Polly says, "but I can't do anything about that. Call me sometime earlier in the day when we can talk."

Deborah wanted badly to tell her sober father how much she appreciated him and the help he gave her during her growing up years while Mother was drinking. "He always told us children we were wonderful and did the best he could under the circumstances." She carefully planned the speech she would make to him while she and he took her young children on a picnic. It didn't go as she envisioned though. As soon as she started speaking, he responded by expressing guilt feelings because he had not done more and because he had not been able to stop the mother's drinking. Deborah had to give up because her statements simply stirred up his guilt. She felt that to pursue the subject would make him feel worse. Although she felt sad that she could not deliver her message, she dropped the matter.

Sometimes, the ACA will have to share those feelings of gratitude toward the sober parent with someone outside the family.

## Develop Positive Addictions

Forrest says that anyone living with a problem drinker can establish a positive addiction that can help alleviate stress, anxiety, and anger. A positive addiction calls for specific, ritualistic, almost compulsive patterns of behavior. Some examples are: meditation, writing, needlepoint, and jogging. When the person maintains the positive addiction, he receives the positive benefits. When he does not keep this routine, anxiety, depression, and irritability set in.

## Enter Self-help Activities

Self-help activities enhance psychological and physical strength. Some examples are dieting, exercising on a regular basis, making new friends and relationships, taking up a hobby, going on vacations, and looking for new ways to enjoy leisure time.

Use your religious faith to help you maintain equilibrium in this situation. Ask your pastor and other Christians to pray for you and your parents. Many Christians fail to reap the benefit of intercessory prayer because they feel ashamed to share the information that they have an alcoholic parent (or spouse). Give others the opportunity to help you carry the load.

## Seek a Support Person

You need a friend who will hear you nonjudgmentally. You might say, for example, "I'm feeling so angry at my drinking parent (or the sober one)."

If the friend gives you a *should* message, such as, "You shouldn't feel that way," or "Well, you just have to not pay attention to what he or she does," that is not good for you. If you are feeling some stirring in your stomach that tells you you are in discomfort, this person is not giving you what you need.

You can tell that person what you need, however. "I need you to just listen to me and accept me for where I am right now, without giving me advice." The friend may think she is doing the right thing by giving advice since that is what is taught in our society. Maybe she never heard that being present with someone has healing power for the person in pain. The friend may be willing to change her responses if you tell her what you need. Or you could tell her how you feel about those responses. "I feel judged when you say that. I need to feel accepted and supported for what I feel and do."

## Work Through Your Anger

One therapist points out that a person can move toward forgiveness, acceptance, and love only after working through one's anger. This will need the help of a professional counselor. Many Christians feel guilty about feeling angry, and they may need the permission of a professional to acknowledge their anger, own it in a nonjudgmental way, and move toward releasing it.

Another therapist said that ACAs feel angry as long as they are fighting reality. They may be denying the reality of their own anger, for example. They may be denying the reality of the parent's drinking. Accepting reality can aid in melting the anger, making room for softer feelings, such as sadness. Once the person moves out of the denial stage, he can begin to make choices about how he will act in the situation.

## Expect Miracles

Since alcohol is a depressant, the drinker becomes depressed. The spouse, living with the problem, becomes depressed. This passes on to all the family members. The ACA can feel hopeless about the future and can expect things to continue to be distressing, which can further fuel the cycle of things causing the distress. The person who is able to maintain some hope and positive attitudes (whether it be a child or a spouse) will come nearer to helping the situation to improve than the one who feels negative. The positive person will relate to the drinker in a different way from the one who feels hopeless.

**Forgiveness**

Gravitz and Bowden say that full recovery for the ACA brings full forgiveness of the parents. They say that it is not necessary to say "I forgive you" directly. The ACA can start thinking of them gently and wishing them well. Perhaps a time will come when he can speak directly to his parents, but if such is not the case, at least the ACA will have taken another step toward personal wholeness.

# 12

# To Joy!

This book has been, admittedly, filled with gloom and doom. We have not been discussing a pretty subject with pleasant happenings. The total picture, however, is not negative. There is hope for you in the future. Cathleen Brooks says that ACAs are fantastic "copers." We can come out of the alcoholic background as extremely skilled persons. We are like cats; if we are thrown, we always land on our feet. Janet Woititz says that if she goes on a speaking engagement and is met at the airport in a blizzard (when all sane people would be at home), she knows that that person is a child of an alcoholic! In one of my workshops, I said, "There are so many of us that, if we organized, we could take over the planet!"

A man asked dourly, "Why should we want to?" Never mind. It is our clout of which I spoke. As mentioned earlier, 80 percent of us go into the helping professions. This planet needs us. If we got well, what would happen to our society? If we formed a political party, our candidate would be a shoo-in. There is nothing we cannot accomplish if we set out minds to it.

# Goals of Recovery

What are the goals of recovery? The following suggestions are not exhaustive, but they are sufficient to get you on your way.

Our overarching goal is to be healed of the wounds from the past. As this process progresses, we want to begin to feel more worthwhile, more hopeful, and to grow in the ability and willingness to care for ourselves and loved ones. We intend to expose and get rid of things that hold us back in life, such as neurotic fears, compulsions, and self-destructive behavior. Last but far from least, we plan to learn to express ourselves more effectively and to develop a larger number of loving relationships.

# Expect Joy!

Cathleen Brooks says, "Let joy be your expectation." Joy was rarely experienced in the alcoholic home and individuals can come out of that home with a "gray" view of life. If they hover above or barely on the survival line, they think that is great and do not expect any more. If they are coping with any degree of efficiency, they consider themselves lucky and do not demand more. Even if their lives are crisis-filled, that is normal, so they may not even know to expect anything different.

Brooks calls us to break whatever bonds bind us to living on a lower level of satisfaction than we, as human beings, are entitled to. Let us expect joy!

The question is, How to get from here to there?

# Stages of Recovery

Herbert Gravitz and Julie Bowden, therapists, have compiled this list of stages of recovery. Check to see where you are. Check periodically to record your progress.

**Survival**

The ACA survived childhood, but at a cost. He is at maximum risk of becoming chemically dependent; of marrying someone who is, or will be, chemically dependent; of developing problematic patterns of behavior in which he gets stuck over and over. He is prone by psychosomatic illnesses, eating disorders, depression, and other problems. Intervention makes him aware of the importance of his past.

**Emergent Awareness**

The person recognizes that something was wrong in childhood and no longer needs to deny it. He acknowledges that past experiences become the key to unlocking the self-validation essential to understanding and coping with present-day life. He shifts from seeing himself as abnormal to identifying himself as an ACA. This ushers in a whirlpool of feelings. *Hope emerges*. He can experience guilt for breaking the family secret. He discovers he is not alone. He can mourn for his lost childhood.

**Core Issues**

Many ACAs do not appear to have problems, but certain personal issues seem to touch nearly all: control; difficulty with trust; avoidance of feelings; overresponsibility and denial of personal needs; all-or-none functioning; dissociation; unconscious, spontaneous age regression; confusion of feeling states; personalizing; adrenalin junkies; and low self-esteem.

**Transformations**

*Change begins with acceptance of the past and is moved forward by an understanding of the past*. Major transformations center around issues of control, all-or-none functioning, trust, and feelings. Increased self-esteem is the by-product.

## Integration

Integration is ushered in as all the disowned parts of the self become more available. No longer does the person think one thing, feel another, and do still a third. Results are increased relaxation and joy. Taking care of self becomes a legitimate pursuit. The ACA moves beyond victimization. Alcoholics must continually live with alcoholism, and ACAs must live with their own history and vulnerability. There is no cure, but there is recovery. This last sentence caused alarm in a fifty-two-year-old client. It struck her as a hopeless position about our personal growth. To me, it would be comparable to learning that one has diabetes. That person must take care of that situation daily for life but it need not devastate the person. We need to keep moving forward in our recovery or we can lose ground.

## Genesis

The spiritual connection complements recovery. Genesis is analogous to the spiritual awakening spoken of in AA. Recovery from alcoholism is threefold: physical, emotional, and spiritual. Therapists believe this is no less true for ACAs. Many ACAs become divorced from their center, or self, very early as a result of their disappointment with God. *Genesis* experiences occur most often toward the end of the recovery process. It is the end that becomes a beginning. It can be a fundamental change in our relationship to ourselves, others, and the universe. In this stage, the ACA usually needs a teacher. In this stage, there is true forgiveness and love.

# Seeking Professional Help

When an ACA enters private counseling or joins a support group, he breaks the three main rules of the home: don't talk, don't feel, and don't trust. The therapeutic setting gives permission to talk, express feelings, and develop trust.

As a person participates in therapy, his perceptions change. He is able to see more clearly what actually happened in the home. For example, he begins to shed his guilt about what took place. He can see his parents through new eyes which brings about new feelings toward them.

After perceptions change, behavior begins to change. The counselee begins to communicate in a new way to himself and to others. He becomes more assertive and stops being a victim. He gets in touch with his power as a person and begins to make more of a contribution to his own life and to the lives of those in his world. His spirituality has new dimensions. Maybe he has had a great deal of anger toward God about what happened. Whatever direction his growth takes, increased spirituality is an inevitable result. Most ACAs return to the faith of their childhood after recovery.

Dr. Claudia Black says that the first important work for ACAs to do is their grief work. She reports that when a counselee reaches the point of crying, she cries so hard she fears she will never stop. The person actually cries about five minutes, Dr. Black observes. It seems forever to the client, but when she stops, much healing has taken place. Probably a professional can help an ACA best with this work.

## Securing Support

An ACA needs a safe support person in his life—someone who will listen nonjudgmentally. If the friend gives you *should* responses, he is not good for your recovery. The five magic words in AA are, "I understand how you feel," and that is true for ACAs.

If you become the support person for someone else, your most valuable contribution is a listening ear and the above statement. In our society, we are raised to believe that the way to help is to give advice. This is incorrect. When someone shares a burden, one of the most frustrating responses that could be given is a *should* response. When I have had a stressful experience, whether great or small, the thing I need most to hear from a listener is something like this: "I'm sure that was difficult for you." People are capable of devising their own solutions for solving their problems; what they need is *support*, not advice.

## Spiritual Support

Pour out your heart to the Lord. Read the entire Book of Psalms over and over. Look for passages where David talked about crying unto the Lord. Underline passages about God's steadfast love. Immerse yourself in the affirmations of God's care. Come to believe that God gives unconditional love rather than the conditional love human beings give.

## Affirm Yourself

Use the book *Daily Affirmations for Adult Children of Alcoholics* by Rokelle Lerner as a guide "for the renewing of your mind." Distortions take place within the perceptions of family members in the alcoholic home—perceptions toward oneself and toward reality, in general. ACAs can have a lot of self-pity. Their self-esteem can be subterranean. They are filled with *should* messages. They feel victims and feel they have no options. They need to put new material into the 'tapes' within their minds.

Write out affirmation statements and repeat them

throughout the day. Here are some examples: I am a person of worth. I can cope. I am OK.

David Semands, author of *Healing for Damaged Emotions* tells that in the British navy, a "still" is blown, just before any combat. A whistle blows and a moment of silence follows. Each person repeats these statements to himself: I am British. I am trained. I can do it.

Dr. Seamands suggests that in a moment of crisis or anxiety we blow the "Christian still." It would go thus: I am a child of God. I am equipped by the Holy Spirit. I can handle whatever comes.

## Expect Miracles

A devotional that I read pointed out that if we start looking for a certain thing, such as the color blue, blue items will start jumping out at us. If we learn a new word, we will hear it again within twenty-four hours because our ears pick it up. Likewise, if we look for miracles, we will see them. Think of the difference within your own mental and physical responses when you think hopefully, prayerfully. Image yourself and your loved ones as whole and healthy emotionally.

## Erase Expectations

This really sounds contradictory to the preceding suggestion! But when people expect certain things to happen, they can set themselves up for disappointment if they do not happen. Frustration, discouragement, and anger can follow. To erase expectations means to accept whatever is happening (acknowledging your powerlessness to change other people and/or situations). Focus on developing a positive attitude. Then, when something good happens, you can receive it as a nice surprise and a miracle. *In everything give thanks*. The human mind cannot think of two things at a time. When you find yourself caught in obsessive thinking, or when the weight of your burdens threatens to overwhelm you, train yourself to give thanks—even for little things. Sometimes ACAs feel that all looks bleak and cannot think of things to be thankful for.

The wife of an active alcoholic attended her first Al-Anon meeting at Thanksgiving. The leader called on each person to tell one thing she was thankful for. When this woman's turn came, she felt so discouraged she said she could not think of anything. "Do you have ingrown toenails?" the leader challenged. The group burst into laughter as the new woman shook her head. "Then give thanks for that!" the leader said. The woman did and joined the others in laughter.

## Cooperate with Nature

*Catecholamines* are biochemicals that the brain secretes when a person is under stress of any type. Catecholamines actually collect within the body, causing physical illnesses. *Endorphins* are the natural tranquilizers and painkillers that the brain secretes when a person experiences pleasure in thought or behavior. Production of endorphins flushes out catecholamines. Do everything you can to increase the flow of endorphins in your system.

Physical exercise, meditation, positive thinking, listening to music, looking at a beautiful picture, focusing on nature as you drive, reading positive and inspirational materials, singing a hymn, reciting affirmative statements mentally, laughing, playing with animals and/or children, doing a hobby, sharing your feelings with another person, and praying are some examples. Whatever brings a pleasurable response for you will produce endorphins. You will feel more relaxed, more positive, and will actually be healthier physically. You will be better able to cope with whatever stresses exist in your life.

Say several peaceful statements to yourself. "Be still" and "I trust in God" are good examples. Notice what happens to your bodily responses when you make those statements. Do you feel yourself getting calmer and more powerful in contrast to feeling out of control and powerless?

Now say, "Things are really hectic." "Everything's a mess." Notice your bodily responses. We can have control over our minds and our bodies by the words and thoughts we put into our minds. Notice the difference in the words *peace* and *panic*. Hearing certain words produces a definite emotional response within. Keep calming statements handy—in writing or in your mind—to pull out when you feel your anxiety levels rising. Put laughter therapy into your daily schedule. Check out books from the library of collections on humor, and laugh for five minutes before going to bed each night.

We cannot control the actions of another person, but we can choose how to think. We can retrain our minds to think positively.

Follow good nutritional guidelines. Many ACAs become addicted to food, sweets, caffeine, or chocolate.

## Choose Faith

Even if it seems as if God is not working in our lives, we have two choices: faith or not faith. We can choose, as an act of the will, to follow faith. Choosing faith is like turning your cup right side up and then looking for God to fill it. What is there to lose? *Repeat the Serenity Prayer.*

"God, grant me the serenity to accept the things I cannot change, courage to change the things I can, and wisdom to know the difference."

Let joy be an expectation! Let us claim the abundant life that Christ came to give.

# Bibliography

## Books

Ackerman, Robert J. *Children of Alcoholics: A Bibliography and Resource Guide*. Indiana, Penn.: Addiction Research Publishing, 1984.

Al-Anon Family Group Headquarters, Inc. *The Dilemma of the Alcoholic Marriage*. Lebanon, Penn.: Sowers Printing Co., 1980.

Beattie, M. *Codependent No More*. Hazelton Foundation, 1987.

Black, Claudia. *It Will Never Happen to Me!* Denver: M.A.C. Printing and Publications Division, 1981.

Colebrook, Joan. "An Australian Childhood," *The New Yorker*, January 21, 1985.

Cork, R. Margaret. The Forgotten Children. Ontario, Canada: PaperJacks, 1980.

Cottle, Thomas J. *Children's Secrets*. Garden City, N.Y.: Anchor Press/Doubleday, 1980.

Forrest, Gary G. *How to Live with a Problem Drinker and Survive*. New York: Atheneum, 1986.

Gravitz, Herbert L. and Julie D. Bowden. *Guide to Recovery: A Book for Adult Children of Alcoholics*.

Holmes Beach, Fla.: Learning Publications, Inc., 1985.

Harris, Thomas A. *I'm O.K.—You're O.K.* New York: Harper & Row, 1969.

Lerner, Rokelle. *Daily Affirmations for Adult Children of Alcoholics*. Pompano Beach, Fla. Health Communications, Inc., 1985. (This book is also available in tapes from the publisher.)

Norwood, R. *Women Who Love Too Much*. Los Angeles: Jeremy Tarcher, Inc., 1985.

Osborne, Cecil G. *Prayer and You*. Waco, Tex.: Word Books, 1974.

Roselline, Gayle and Mark Word. *Of Course, You're Angry*. Center City, Minn.: Hazelden Foundation, 1985.

Sanford, Agnes. *The Healing Light*. New York: Ballantine Books, 1983.

Schaef, Anne Wilson. *Co-Dependence: Misunderstood - Mistreated*. Minneapolis: Winston Press, Inc., 1986.

Seamands, David A. *Healing for Damaged Emotions*. Wheaton, Ill.: Victor Books, 1984.

Seixas, Judith S. and Geralding Youcha. *Children of Alcoholism: A Survivor's Guide*. New York: Crown Publishers, 1985.

Walters, Richard P. *Anger: Yours & Mine & What to Do About It*. Grand Rapids, Mich.: Zondervan Publishing House, 1981.

Wegscheider, Sharon. *Another Chance: Hope and Health for the Alcoholic Family*. Palo Alto, Calif.: Science and Behavior Books, Inc., 1981.

Wegscheider-Cruse, Sharon. *Choice-Making*. Pompano Beach, Fla.: Health Communications, Inc., 1985.

Woititz, J. *Adult Children of Alcoholics*. Pompano Beach, Fla.: Health Communications, 1985.

# Films

*Children of Denial*. A filmed presentation by Claudia

Black describing the problems and feelings of young, adolescent, and adult children of alcoholics. Contact ACT, P. O. Box 8536, Newport Beach, Calif. 92660.

*Another Chance.* This film focuses on the anguish and ultimate emotional breakthrough of an adult child of an alcoholic who experiences the "reconstruction" process.

*Family Trap.* This film explores the roles played by members of an alcoholic family. Contact: Health Communications, 2119-A Hollywood Blvd., Hollywood, Fla. 33020.

## To Get More Help

Al-Anon/Alateen Family Group Headquarters, Inc.
Madison Square Station
New York, N. Y. 10010
(212) 683-1771

Alcoholics Anonymous World Services, Inc.
468 Park Ave. S.
New York, N. Y. 10016
(212) 686-1100

National Association for Children of Alcoholics
31706 Coast Highway, Suite 201
South Laguna, Calif. 92677
(714) 499-3889

National Council on Alcoholism
12 W. 21st St.
New York, N. Y. 10010
(212) 206-6770

National Clearinghouse for Alcohol Information
P. O. Box 1908
Rockville, Md. 20850
(301) 468-2600

## ABOUT THE AUTHOR

SARA HINES MARTIN is a staff member at Northeast Counseling Center, Marietta, Georgia. She is an adult child of an alcoholic. Martin leads workshops and support groups for ACAs and does extensive private counseling. She received her education at Carson-Newman (B.A.), Southwestern Seminary (M.R.E.), and Georgia State University (M.S.). In addition, Martin has studied at the School of Pastoral Care, North Carolina Baptist Hospital, Winston-Salem, North Carolina.

Straightforward, authoritative guides to alcohol abuse for those who suffer as well as family and friends.

# BANTAM'S BESTSELLING BOOKS ON ADDICTION AND RECOVERY

## ADDICTION

The most up-to-date information from leading experts in the field

☐ **800-COCAINE**, Mark S. Gold, M.D.

34388-2 $3.95/$4.95 in Canada

☐ **THE FACTS ABOUT DRUGS AND ALCOHOL**, Mark S. Gold, M.D.

27826-6 $3.95/$4.95 in Canada

☐ **UNDER THE INFLUENCE: A Guide to the Myths and Realities of Alcoholism**, James R. Milam, Ph.D., and Katherine Ketcham

27487-2 $4.95/$5.95 in Canada

## RECOVERY

Books that offer concrete tools for physical,
emotional, and spiritual recoveery

☐ **LIVING ON THE EDGE: A Guide to Intervention for Families with Druga nd Alcohol Problems**, Katherine Ketcham and Ginny Lyford Gustafson 34606-2 $7.95/$9.95 in Canada

☐ **RECOVERING: How to Get and Stay Sober**, L. Ann Mueller, M.D.,m and Katherine Ketcham

34303-3 $9.95/$12.95 in Canada

☐ **TURNABOUT: New Help for the Woman Alcoholic**, Jean Kirkpatrick, Ph.D. 34860-4 $8.95/$11.95 in Canada

☐ **THE TWELVE STEPS REVISITED,**Ronald L. Rogers, Chandler Scott McMillin, and Morris A. Hill

34733-0 $8.50/$11.50 in Canada

☐ **RESTORE YOUR LIFE: A Living Plan for Sober People,** Anne Geller, M.D. with M.J. Territo

07153-X $21.95/$26.95 in Canada (hardcover)

☐ **RELAPSE TRAPS: How To Avoid the 12 Most Common Pitfalls in Recovery**, Ronald L. Rogers and Chandler Scott McMillin 35479-5 $9.50/$12.50 in Canada

☐ **IN STEP WITH GOD: A Scriptural Guide for Twelve Step Programs,** Paul Barton Doyle and John Ishee

29292-7 $3.99/$4.99 in Canada

☐ **DON'T HELP: A Positive Guide to Working with the Alcoholic**, Ronald L. Rogers and Chandler Scott McMillin

34716-0 $8.95/$11.95 in Canada

## ADULT CHILDREN

Essential reading for the millions who grew up in
dysfunctional families.

☐ **THE ADULT CHILDREN OF ALCOHOLICS SYNDROME**, Wayne Kritsberg 27279-9 $4.50/$5.50 in Canada

☐ **BECOMING YOUR OWN PARENT: The Solution for Adult Children of Alcoholic and Other Dysfunctional Families,** Dennis Wholey    34788-8 $9.95/$12.95 in Canada
☐ **HEALING FOR ADULT CHILDREN OF ALCOHOLICS,** Sara Hines Martin    28246-8 $4.50/$5.50 in Canada

## FAMILY ISSUES

Groundbreaking books on conquering co-dependence
and helping addicted family members.

☐ **LOVING AN ALCOHOLIC: Help and Hope for Co-dependents,** Jack Mumey    27236-5 $4.95/$5.95 in Canada
☐ **TOXIC PARENTS: Overcoming Their Hurtful Legacy and Reclaiming YOur Life,** Dr. Susan Forward with Craig Buck
    28434-7 $5.95/$6.95 in Canada

## HEALING RELATIONSHIPS

Books that point readers toward a healthier self and
new ways of relating with others.

☐ **HOW TO BREAK YOUR ADDICTION TO A PERSON,** Howard M. Halpern, Ph.D.    26005-7 $4.95/$6.50 in Canada
☐ **OUT OF DARKNESS INTO THE LIGHT: A Journey of Inner Healing,** Gerald G. Jampolsky, M.D.  34791-8 $6.95/$8.95 in Canada

## MEDITATIONALS

Daily inspiration and guidance based on the 12-step programs

☐ **A NEW DAY: 365 Meditations for Personal and Spiritual Growth,** Anonymous    34591-5 $6.95/$8.95 in Canada
☐ **FAMILY FEELINGS: Daily Meditations for Healthy Relationships,** Martha Vanceburg and Sylvia Silverman
    34705-5 $6.95/$8.95 in Canada
☐ **FEEDING THE SOUL: Daily Meditations for Recovering from Eating Disorders,** Caroline Adams Miller
    35279-2 $8.00/$10.00 in Canada

---

# We Deliver!
## And So Do These Bestsellers.